FOCUS ON

BIRDWATCHING

ROB HUME

HAMLYN

ACKNOWLEDGEMENTS

The publishers would like to thank the British Library of Wildlife Sounds for the loan of the recording equipment shown on pp 40, Canon (UK) Ltd for the photographic equipment on pp 28-29, Mirador for the birdwatching items on pp 10-11, and Andrew Cleave for the loan of specimens on pp 31, 50 and 61; and the following individuals and organizations for permission to produce the pictures in this book:

David Johnson (studio photography for Octopus Publishing Group): front cover (border), 10-11, 12-13, 17, 25, 26, 28-29, 30, 40, 50, 61. Heather Angel: 12 top.
Aquila Photographics: S. C. Brown 22 bottom, J. F. Carlyon 52 right, Peter Castell 45 top right, Steve Chambers 37 bottom, Anthony Cooper 68, Hanne and Jens Eriksen 57 top, Hans Gebuis 14 bottom, 51 left, 57 bottom, Mike Lane 14 top, Wayne Lankinen 9 bottom left, 16 top right, 17 top, 55 top, Robert Maier 27, Richard T. Mills 44 top and bottom left, 55 bottom, 74 left. Mike Mockler 75 left, Alan Richards 22 top, M. C. Wilkes 18 top right, 38 top right, 69. Biofotos: Andrew Henley 16 left.
Bruce Coleman Ltd: Gordon Langsbury 16-17; Eric and David Hosking 18 centre right, 33 top, 62 top, 63.
Frank Lane Picture Agency: W. S. Clark 9 top left, Desmond Dugan 42 left, David T. Grewcock 37 top and centre, A. R. Hamblin 15, 50 left, 52 left, 60, Peggy Heard 8 bottom, S. D. K. Maslowski 33 bottom, Francois Merlet 45 bottom right, W. T. Miller 30 centre, Philip Perry 30 top, Fritz Polking 29 right, 58 left, Leonard Lee Rue 42 right, Silvestris Fotoservice 45 centre right, R. Van Nostrand 9 top right, Martin B. Withers 56 bottom.
NHPA: Bruce Beehler 38 left, Melvin Grey 38 bottom right, Hellio and Van Ingen 19, Stephen Krasemann 54, Roger Tidman 23. Nature Photographers Ltd: Frank V. Blackburn 44 right, Kevin Carlson 35 right, Colin Carver 41, 58 right, Bob Chapman 74 right, Thomas Ennis 30 bottom, M. P. Harris 9 bottom right, E. A Janes 29 top left, 35 left, Philip J. Newman 32, 75 right, Paul Sterry title page, 8 top, 29 top centre, 34 left, 36, 51 right, 62 bottom, 65, Roger Tidman 21, 24, 34 right, 39, 45 left, 49, 52-53, 56 top. RSPB: M. W. Richards 16 bottom right.
ZEFA 18 bottom left, 46-47, 64.

Illustrators:
David Ashby (Garden Studio): 11, 15, 19, 20-21, 23, 41, 63, 64. Peter Bull Art: 22, 24, 27 (bottom), 39 (top), 43 (top), 43 (right), 51 (top), 53, 54-55, 56, 59 (bottom), 60, 66 (bottom left), 67 (top right), 67 (bottom right). Malcolm Ellis (Bernard Thornton Artists): 46-47, 72-73, 74. Ian Lewington: 34-35, 35, 45, 57, 58-59 (top), 65, 66-67 (main). Mick Loates (Linden Artists): 9, 32-33, 36-37, 39 (bottom), 48-49. Robert Morton (Bernard Thornton Artists): 43 (bottom left), 51 (bottom), 68-69, 70-71. John Rignall (Linden Artists): 26-27

Editor: Andrew Farrow
Series Designer: Anne Sharples
Picture Researcher: Judy Todd
Production Controller: Linda Spillane

Published in 1992 by
Hamlyn Children's Books,
Part of Reed International Books,
Michelin House, 81 Fulham Road,
London SW3 6RB

ISBN 0 600 57366 4

Printed in Great Britain

CONTENTS

BIRDS, BIRDS, BIRDS

The very earliest birds probably developed from small, ancient dinosaurs. Thus they have been around for millions of years, longer than humans. But what makes them special? They are warmblooded, which makes them like mammals. They all lay eggs - but so do reptiles and amphibians. Most of them fly - but so do insects and bats. The unique thing about a bird is its feathers.

Feathers are strong, but very lightweight. They give birds a smooth shape, and create the aerofoil shape of the wings that lets birds fly. They also fit tightly together in a waterproof covering.

BIRDS ARE EVERYWHERE

Birds have developed ways of life that let them live practically anywhere there is something to eat and a safe place for them to rest.

Some fly over Mount Everest and over the middle of the biggest oceans. They can fly to over 7,000 metres in the air and can dive to 300 metres deep in the sea. They have even been seen over the South Pole. Some species, or types, of bird are amazingly rare: only 10 or fewer individuals survive in the whole world. Others are very common, with many millions alive at any one time. There are familiar ones, such as sparrows, that live close to man; whereas in the forests of Peru, several birds were seen by scientists for the very first time in the 1980s. There are very probably some not yet discovered.

BIRDWATCHING

Birds are the most attractive and most easily seen animals on Earth. For anyone wanting to enjoy the fascination of natural history, they are the best subject to watch and study. There are around 9,200 species of birds in the world. South America has the richest variety, but there are over 800 species seen regularly in North America and 500 in Europe.

Some of the most exciting sights in the natural world are huge gatherings of birds. Gannets (above) nest in vast, noisy colonies; and other seabirds, such as kittiwakes and guillemots, crowd together in gigantic, noisy 'cities' on sheer cliffs above the sea.

The house sparrow (above) is a common European bird. It was taken abroad by early explorers and now lives in America and Australia too. In Egypt it has followed man across the desert and lives in tiny settlements where it can find a few scraps. In the USA the starling, also taken from Europe to a country where there were no starlings, is extremely common.

LIVES OF EXTREMES

Birds can survive in quite extreme conditions. The roadrunner in a hot desert (top left) may seek shade, and ruffle its feathers in a cooling breeze in temperatures over 40°C. But it also puts up with an overnight freeze. Penguins (bottom right) survive on the ocean and in bleak, windswept places with the worst weather on earth. Dense, fur-like feathers and a thick layer of fat keep them warm. Cactus wrens hop about in cactus and semi-desert scrub (bottom left). Tropical pittas (top right) live all their lives in the gloom at the base of dense, wet jungle. They are colourful but are difficult to find.

The California condor is nearly extinct. It is one of the rarest, as well as one of the largest, birds in the world. There are none left alive in the wild, but about 40 in zoos. The hope is to release young ones from the zoos back into the wild.

LEARNING TO WATCH

If you want to learn how to watch birds, this book should point you in the right direction. But birdwatching is a very practical hobby, and so you will need to get out and about, watching and learning.

One of the most worthwhile things you can do is join a well-organized society or naturalists' trust. Most experienced birdwatchers will be pleased to help you learn more, and they can advise you on the best, and safest, locations. One of the most important organizations is the Royal Society for the Protection of Birds, The Lodge, Sandy, Bedfordshire, SG19 2DL. The RSPB has many local groups throughout Britain. In Australia, there is the Royal Ornithologists' Union, 21 Gladstone St, Mooneeyponds, Victoria 3039, which publishes *The Emu*; and in Canada, there's the Canadian Nature Federation, 453 Sussex Drive, Ottawa, Ontario, KIN 6Z4.

SPOTTER'S HINT
The best birdwatcher is a sensible birdwatcher. Never go out alone; and always tell someone responsible where you are going, and how long you will be. Never visit dangerous places, such as cliff-tops.

EQUIPMENT

The essential piece of birdwatching equipment is a pair of binoculars. You really get what you pay for, but there is no need to pay *very* high prices for famous makes. Of course, don't buy poor-quality binoculars with lenses that distort shapes or colour.

BINOCULARS

Binoculars are described with numbers: 8 X 30, 10 X 50 and so on. The first number is the magnification - things look eight or 10 times bigger, or whatever the figure is. Go for anything between seven and 10, *no more*. The second figure is the width of the big lens in millimetres. The bigger that this lens is, the brighter the view, but the binoculars are also bigger and heavier. Try 7 X 50, 8 X 30, 8 X 40 and 10 X 40 and see what suits you best. Small, light binoculars are far better than great big heavy ones, which will make your arms tired and wobble as you look through them.

Fold-down rubber eyecups are useful for people who wear glasses - they help bring the lenses closer to your eyes and give a wider field of view.

Roof-prism binoculars are small and light, but good ones are also expensive.

A clamp or tripod head allows a telescope to be locked into position or swung to follow a moving bird.

Normal binoculars are used by most people but can be difficult for small hands.

TELESCOPES

Telescopes can magnify birds over 20 times. But they may be no good for watching birds close to, or in dense trees or bushes, because the magnification is too high - the telescope will not focus close enough and the area seen is too small.

Good telescopes are 'spotting scopes' or 'prismatic scopes', which really need to be on a tripod or clamp to keep them steady. Go for one with a lens at least 60mm across. Ask a dealer for advice, and try out several before you buy.

You use a telescope with one eye. You can learn to keep the other open, or close it, or cover it with a hand. Either way, relax the eye you look with and don't strain - otherwise you might see double when you stop!

A prismatic telescope has a 'stepped' shape near the end.

IN THE FIELD

On a cold day, it's a good idea to take your binoculars out of their case a while before you start birdwatching, so they will warm up and won't steam up when you use them. Try not to breathe on the lenses.

If you look down at your binoculars and swing them around to find a bird, you will probably miss it. Instead, when you see the bird, keep your eyes up, looking at it, and raise your binoculars to your eyes. Practise until your aim is perfect.

Always keep binoculars clean. Blow away dust and dirt, and wipe with a soft, dry, clean cloth only when you are sure there's no grit on the lenses - otherwise you will have scratches that ruin them! But keep them on the strap around your neck when you walk - a drop or bump will ruin them, too.

SPOTTER'S HINT
Never look at the sun with binoculars or a telescope - if you do, you will blind yourself. As you walk, try to keep to a route that means you see most birds out of the line of the sun.

USING BINOCULARS

You will be able to see birds most clearly if you balance the difference between your eyes, by using the adjustable eyepiece. To do so, look at a distant pole or tree. Cover the right lens, then focus the left with the central wheel.

Next, cover the left lens. Look through the right one, and make the image appear sharp using only the adjustable eyepiece - don't touch the central wheel. Relax your eyes and let the adjustment focus for you. Now both eyes will be focused.

Don't touch the eyepiece again - just focus with the central wheel when you see birds close up or far away. If your binoculars will not focus properly, or get damaged, don't try to fix them yourself: get an expert to repair them.

CLOTHING

The kind and colour of clothes matter less than their function. As you'll see, experienced birdwatchers know that the day is much more enjoyable if they are comfortable and dry, rather than dressed for fashion. Having said that, there is no need at all on a warm, sunny day to dress like a birdwatcher going to the Arctic! Then, a subdued T-shirt and jeans are fine. There's no need to 'look the part'.

WARM AND DRY

Getting cold and wet is miserable, and can even be dangerous in exposed places. On a cold day, wear layers of sweaters rather than just one thick jacket. On top, wear a waterproof jacket with a tough outer layer - choose one that has plenty of big pockets for your gloves, notebook and field guides.

Waterproof overtrousers are heavy and clumsy, but sometimes you need them. Lightweight ones are often not very waterproof, but they do keep out cold winds. On your feet, rubber boots are the real answer in very wet ground, but many people prefer to wear trainers everywhere. Don't forget gloves and a hat. You lose an awful lot of heat through your head, and, even if you don't like hats, a simple woolly one is vital if the weather should turn really bad.

FED AND WATERED

When you are out you are bound to get hungry and need a drink. Food and drink may seem heavy but you will be ready for them after a few hours. Food is easy - take whatever you like!

Birds see well anyway, so the colour of your clothes is not too important - a green jacket is not much better than a blue one. But you should avoid bright orange or yellow, and especially white. Try to blend in if you can, but keeping still and quiet is just as important as wearing camouflaged battle-dress.

FIELD GUIDES

When choosing a field guide, look for one with clearly-presented pictures of the birds. Why not compare some of the pictures with common birds you can watch near your home, and see if they are good likenesses of them?

SPOTTER'S HINT
Remember, if you are eating sandwiches (or sticky cakes), don't drop crumbs all over your binocular eyepieces. They make a real mess and will ruin your view of the next rare bird.

READ ABOUT IT

You can't beat expert tuition when learning about birds, but the next best thing is a good book. Get a good field guide which illustrates and describes the birds clearly. For your main book, go for one with good paintings, because photographs of birds are often misleading. There are some useful magazines, too. You can get ones from the main organizations on subscription, such as the monthly *Birds*, from the Royal Society for the Protection of Birds; and *Bird Life*, from the junior section of the RSPB, versions of which are published around the world. And high street bookstalls have other magazines.

You can ask at your library where to find a local bird report. This will show what birds have been seen in your area, year by year. It will also help you to find out some good places to see birds.

PERMITS AND PERMISSION

Most land is private, so you'll need to know where you are allowed to go. One way of finding out is by looking at the annual *Birdwatchers' Yearbook*, which gives full details of reserves, addresses and, just as important, how to obtain permits allowing you to visit certain sites. Fortunately, many national nature reserves have free access all the time, and most country parks are always open. However, permits are needed for many other places.

The RSPB reserves and those of other major organizations are mostly open all the time, but they may charge a fee to non-members. Local reserves often require a permit from the local wildlife trust or other society. Whatever you do, don't just assume you can wander in, and certainly do not trespass - on a reserve, on farmland, or anywhere else.

LEAFLETS
Leaflets and brochures about birdwatching sites are essential for planning a visit. Always check the opening times *before* you go.

MAPS
A good 1:50,000-scale map is invaluable for finding footpaths, woods and even telephone boxes. A compass might be needed if you are going on longer walks. You should visit remote areas only if you are with someone who knows the area well.

NOTEBOOK AND PENCIL
Don't forget to take a notebook and pencil: not even experienced birdwatchers remember everything they see!

BACK GARDEN BIRDING

There are many species of bird that you will never see without travelling to the right kind of habitat. But there are many times when you can't travel, or the weather is so bad that you don't want to. Bringing birds to you is the answer!

GARDEN BIRDS

Garden birds are just as interesting as woodland ones. In fact, most are species that live in woods and clearings, and move into new habitats when suitable back yards with plenty of trees and lawns are planted. Many back gardens are, to birds, just like woodland glades. With a bit of thought and effort, the clever birdwatcher can make them even better.

ALL MODERN CONVENIENCES

Birds need four things that gardens can supply. They need a safe place to nest. They need somewhere safe and warm to roost each night. They need food. And they need water to drink and to bathe in.

A PLACE TO NEST

Nesting places depend on the kind of bird. For some birds you can put up a nestbox. Others will never use a box, but would appreciate a good, thick, evergreen bush or thorn hedge. You can plant dense shrubs and surround them with spiky thorn or gorse to keep out any marauding cats.

Roost sites are really much the same as nest sites. Any kind of thick, dark, sheltered shrubbery will help birds find a good place for the night, away from prowling cats and owls and out of the cold wind.

Firecrests (rare but regular in the UK and commoner over most of Europe) love thick evergreens, whether holly, evergreen oaks or conifers. Not only do they nest and feed in them, but the dense foliage gives them a safe, dry, sheltered place to get a good night's sleep.

A box attracts birds to nest and lay eggs. It would be unfair on the birds if you lured them to a spot where cats could catch them, or into a poor-quality box that fell apart after a wet day.

Make sure the box is strongly built, and put it in a safe place.

SIMPLE BIRD BOXES

A bird box is fun to watch. The diagrams show two kinds made from planks about 15mm thick - the open-fronted box will appeal more to wrens and flycatchers. Make sure the hole is neither too small nor too large - about 25mm for blue and coal tits, 28mm for great tits. Keep the box out of reach of people who might want to look inside or take the eggs. And put it where cats will have a job to reach it.

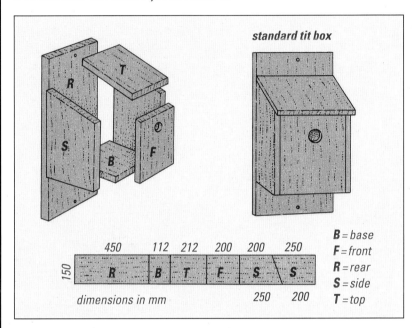

standard tit box

450	112	212	200	200	250	
R	B	T	F	S	S	150
				250	200	

dimensions in mm

B = base
F = front
R = rear
S = side
T = top

Purple martins in the USA live in amazing bird 'towers', with many boxes built up together on top of a stout pole. Purple martins are unusually gregarious and like to live in such tight groups. In Europe house martins nest close together, but in mud nests built under the eaves of houses. You can make or buy artificial house martin nests which attract birds to build their own alongside.

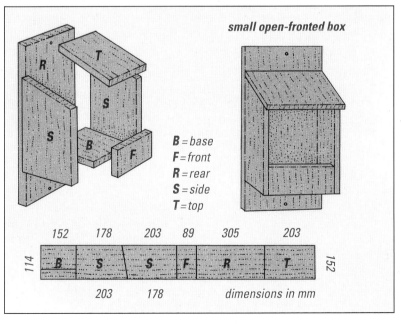

small open-fronted box

B = base
F = front
R = rear
S = side
T = top

152	178	203	89	305	203	
B	S	S	F	R	T	152
114						
	203	178		dimensions in mm		

HOUSE MARTIN HOMES

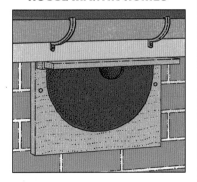

An artificial nest can be used to mimic the mud nest that house martins build. It can be made from papier-mâché or gummed paper, though waterproof glue and paint is essential!

FOOD AND DRINK

Providing food is simple, and is the easiest way to get birds to come close. A feeder station or bird table is ideal for attracting birds in larger numbers. It is best not to supply artificial food in late spring or summer, as it may harm young birds being fed in the nest.

Water is no problem, either. A bird bath, an old dish, a tray sunk into the lawn, all make simple water containers. A properly constructed pond, with plants, is really the ideal, if you have enough space.

A VITAL SUPPLY

Birds drink a lot, especially those that eat dry seeds and nuts from feeders. They also need to bathe to keep their feathers in good condition. So they need water to splash in, even in the coldest winter weather. Make sure that you keep a small pool or bird bath free of ice each day so the birds, such as this small finch, can drink and splash in it (but never use antifreeze, which will kill them).

A bird table is just a square of wood on top of a post. A roof is not necessary, but makes it look better. Raised strips around the edge help keep the food on in a wind. You just need to put out kitchen scraps - cake crumbs, uncooked pastry, cheese, fat, bits of bread, dried fruit - then sit back and watch the show.

OBSERVING GARDEN BIRDS

Try taking detailed notes on your garden birds. The facts you collect will be fascinating and may change over the years. First, keep a list of the maximum number at a time of each species you see, and note down what they feed on. Give them plenty of food options, and try several feeders.

In America, the black-capped chickadee (left), and in Europe, the greenfinch (centre) are two birds that will come readily to food put out in the garden. The yellow warbler (right) is not a feeder bird, but will come into American gardens with large orchards

SOME THINGS TO LOOK FOR

How many species take food that you put out? How many refuse it, but eat only natural food in the garden? Are there flocks of bird table and feeder visitors, but just ones and twos of the natural feeders - or is it the other way around? And do birds spend time fighting for food or eating quietly together?

Does this change in really cold or snowy weather, when the birds may get down to more serious eating to stay alive? Are there more males than females? Look at your notes to see if this stays the same in autumn, winter and spring. Maybe the numbers of different species change as the seasons go by. Who knows what you might discover!

TEMPTING FEEDERS

Sometimes, new bird tables are sold complete with a bird nestbox on top. These are hopeless. Birds trying to feed chase off the nesters. Birds trying to nest spend all their time trying to chase off the feeders. It is a poor idea! Go for the simple ones all the time.

Put grated cheese on the ground below your feeders. This helps the smaller birds that don't use bird tables and often get chased off by the rest. Try natural bird food, too: why not plant some snowberries, pyracantha, cotoneaster, mezereon and other bushes that grow succulent berries?

Why not try other feeder ideas? A bag of nuts or scraps is easy to hang - red plastic bags full of peanuts seem to attract siskins - or you can buy a wire-mesh nut basket. Try two or three scattered about the garden, to give several birds the chance to feed.

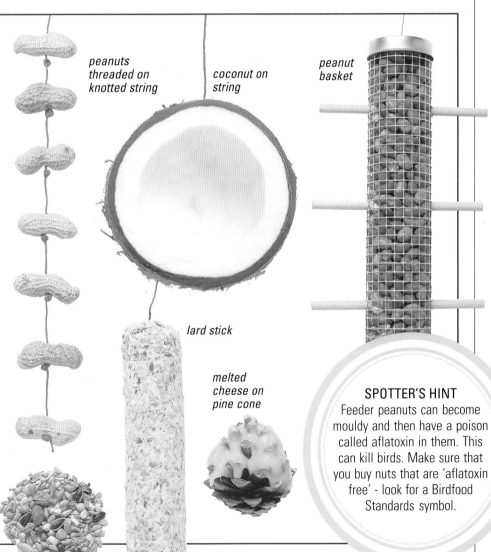

peanuts threaded on knotted string

coconut on string

peanut basket

lard stick

melted cheese on pine cone

mixed seeds

SPOTTER'S HINT
Feeder peanuts can become mouldy and then have a poison called aflatoxin in them. This can kill birds. Make sure that you buy nuts that are 'aflatoxin free' - look for a Birdfood Standards symbol.

SPECIAL GARDEN BIRDS

Some garden birds can be very special, because they are rare or because they are very colourful. And you never know what bird might visit. It really is exciting to see something a little unusual from your own window. Watch early in the morning, before there are people about, and you may be surprised at what birds you see. If you have space, make a pond and see even more birds come to drink and bathe.

SWEET ATTRACTION

In the summer in the USA, special bottles of sugar and water with tiny dripping spouts may bring in hummingbirds, fabulous little birds that look like they should be in the tropical forests. The same nectar feeders will bring orioles into gardens in Texas. In other parts of the world, long, narrow troughs are filled with a sugary solution, attracting a variety of nectar-eating birds in larger numbers.

In Europe, redwings visit gardens in cold weather - they love juicy berries.

Northern cardinals are spectacular visitors to United States gardens.

GARDEN SPECIALS

In Europe, clever use of feeders and nestboxes can attract maybe 20 or 30 species in a good garden, including some special birds. Bushes with berries lasting through the winter are great for less-common visitors from the north, such as fieldfares and redwings coming in when the weather is bad. Very special visitors in some years are waxwings, pushed out from Scandinavia by bad weather and a lack of food.

In the USA, eastern bluebirds and blue jays are wonderfully colourful. Look out, too, in winter for tufted titmice flocks roaming through wooded gardens. Woodpeckers come to take nuts and seeds, and red-headed and downy woodpeckers are quite frequent. American robins feed under bird tables.

Few birds in the USA give such a thrill as hummingbirds, which feed from flowers but will dart in to a special feeder.

A VARIED MENU

Experiment with different foods to attract a special selection of birds. For example, cheese and suet will attract great spotted woodpeckers. Cheese rubbed into cracks in tree bark can be found by treecreepers and long-tailed tits, which rarely come to bird tables. Drill holes in a thick stick, fill them with food, and hang the stick from a branch.

Peanuts in mesh feeders, too, are good for attracting interesting birds. In England, nuthatches will come from nearby woods. In Scotland there are no nuthatches, but even the much rarer crested tit sometimes comes to gardens from its normal habitat, the Scots pine forest.

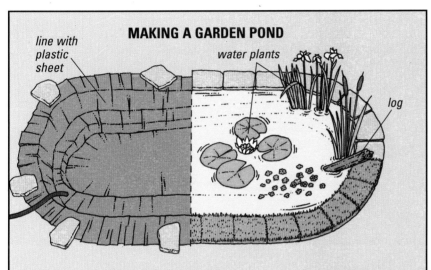

MAKING A GARDEN POND

line with plastic sheet

water plants

log

A garden pond should be deep at one end and shallow at the other, and without steep banks, so birds can stand at the edge and drink and bathe. A branch or ramp can help them get at the water.

A kestrel may visit a garden to catch a sparrow or vole.

GARDEN HUNTERS

Sometimes birds of prey will take advantage of the congregation of small birds at a feeder. A sparrowhawk may sweep through a garden at great speed, causing a mass panic. If it has been quick enough, it may have caught an unlucky sparrow or a finch. If not, it may try again later, when the birds have settled down. You soon learn the alarm notes of the birds when a hawk is about. Tits give a high, thin squeak; starlings a sharp, quick 'tick' call.

OTHER NESTBOXES

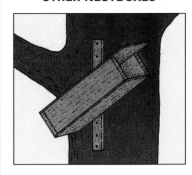

A long, sloping 'box' firmly wired to a big tree will mimic a broken, hollow branch and maybe attract a pair of owls to come and nest.

Woodpeckers usually chisel out their own holes, but will use a box filled with polystyrene or balsa wood so they can dig out the right size cavity.

Swifts nest in holes under roofs. You can maybe persuade someone to build a large swift box into your house by taking out a brick and putting in a board with a suitable entrance slit.

FIELDCRAFT AND HIDES

Birds have strong eyesight and good hearing. They are under such constant threat from predators that they are always alert and ready to fly off at the first hint of danger. Therefore, to get to see them well, the birdwatcher has to be careful, and clever.

KEEP YOUR EYES PEELED

If you want to see birds, don't talk about something else and look at the ground. Keep looking around you, because you will find birds by noticing tiny movements, hearing small sounds, even seeing the shadows from birds overhead. Look around, look back, and look up.

KEEP QUIET

No-one wants birdwatching to be unfriendly and boring, and going out with friends is nearly always most enjoyable and safest. But there are times when it does no good to be talking and laughing when you really want to be getting closer to the birds. You just have to be quiet so you don't scare away the birds, and can hear bird calls, too. Then you can track them down more easily. You can hear birds calling much better if you stop for a moment than while you are walking along. Stop, look and listen!

Loud, hissing 'whispers' carry as far as ordinary talk, so be really quiet if you are getting in close.

SIMPLE FIELDCRAFT TECHNIQUES

ANTICIPATION

If you see a break in the landscape, be ready to look there for birds. They are often found at the edge of a wood, or where a track passes through a forest. So, whenever you walk up to an 'edge' of any kind, such as a ditch or stream, go very slowly, quietly, and look both ways. Remember, though, it is not always possible to get the best position to watch birds - just try your best, and enjoy the challenge of seeing as much as possible.

USING COVER

Make the maximum use of any available cover to conceal yourself from birds. If you are walking in open countryside, try not to break cover and be highlighted against the sky: it's better to look around bushes and hedges, rather than over them. That way, birds are less likely to spot you. You can hide in bushes and hedges, or back up against them so that your shape doesn't stand out from the surroundings. Leaning on a tree will help to steady your binoculars.

USING BINOCULARS

You can keep your binoculars steady by propping a finger or thumb against your face or chin. When it is windy, you can squat or sit, then rest your elbows on your knees. You may have to lie down to get out of the wind.

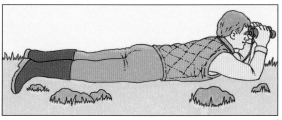

THE SUN AT YOUR BACK

You will see colours better with the sun behind you rather than in front of you - most birds look black against a bright, sunlit sky. Also, it can be very difficult to see birds on rivers and lakes if the sun is reflecting from the surface. But you can often spot a bird in thick foliage by looking up through the leaves against a bright sky and seeing the bird in silhouette. Then you can walk round to get a better view of it, with the light behind you.

KEEP STILL

Birds are especially good at noticing movement. If you keep still, even the sharpest-eyed bird may not recognize you. But make the slightest movement or sound, and it will be gone.

Always keep your actions to a minimum. Be slow and smooth when you move, pausing often, and be relaxed. If you can't find any cover when stalking birds, crouch down and move steadily forwards. Birds may not notice a direct approach so soon as a sideways movement.

Pointing out birds to other people is not as easy as it might seem. Try to use fixed landmarks ('left of the church tower') or use the 'clock' system ('four o'clock from the boathouse').

DON'T TRY TOO HARD

Remember, other people may be looking at the same bird as you. There is really no need to get so close that you scare it away. That may not help the bird, and you will lose friends, too.

You should also take care when pointing with your hands, if you don't want to speak aloud: bare hands are pale and easy to see, and birds will soon notice quick movements.

SPOTTER'S HINT
Before setting out on a birdwatching trip, check the local weather forecast. Small birds will stay in cover if there are strong winds.

LURING BIRDS

Some birdwatchers use tape recordings of owls to lure other birds within watching range. They make hissing sounds - 'pishing' - and 'squeak' by sucking the backs of their hands. These strange noises make other birds come to investigate, thinking there's an owl about. Even if these sounds *are* owl-like, they are often overdone by birdwatchers, and the birds get bored - or they simply move off because they are too disturbed. So, if you try these techniques, don't use them more than you really have to.

Cars make good hides if you keep still and quiet. You can buy a window clamp for a telescope.

OBSERVING A WADER ROOST

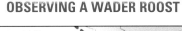

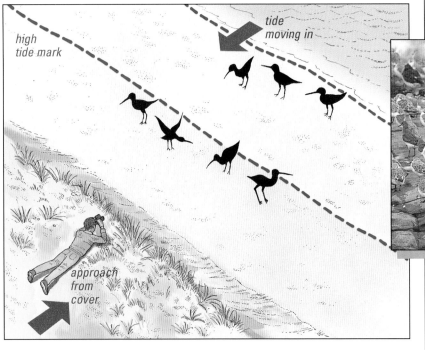

high tide mark

tide moving in

approach from cover

Waders, such as these sanderlings and dunlins, must roost in peace at high tide. Sanderlings need to feed well and double their weight before they fly on to their breeding grounds.

SHORELINE SPECTACULARS

High-tide roosts of wading birds are fascinating to see. But the birds need security and rest. It is your responsibility to enjoy them while not scaring them off, because when the tide is high they will have nowhere else to go.

Shorebirds feed on the mud when the tide is low, and they can be a very long way from footpaths and safe shores. The best way to see them is to wait until the tide rises and they come closer. Find a tide table for the place you are visiting. Time your visit for the two or three hours before high tide. Find a comfortable, safe spot (where you won't get cut off by a rising tide) and sit still, low down against a bank or hedge. Keep down below the sky, and wait until the birds come to you - a lot of patience is needed. And don't get up and leave when they have all turned up to sleep. You need to let the tide turn before you have to move and disturb the birds.

FIXED HIDES

Most nature reserves have fixed hides made of wood. They are good for getting out of sight, so you can stretch and relax without frightening birds away.

A fixed hide is also a hollow, noisy 'box', and there is no excuse to talk loudly, or stick your hands out of the slots. Keep your hands and telescope inside if you can.

You may find the seats too high or too low. Standing or kneeling may be better than sitting. With a telescope, you may have to stand up at the back to use it, or remove it from its tripod to balance it on the ledge in front.

Many reserves have fixed, wooden hides. They are put in the best places for birdwatching, and are relatively comfortable.

BUILDING A HIDE

keep cloth covering tight

twine

hole for camera and binoculars, covered by flaps

some local vegetation breaks the outline

stout wooden or light metal frame

guy ropes to keep hide upright

entry flap

Making a basic hide is quite easy. You need stout wood for a frame, some rope and tent pegs to hold it in place, and some kind of canvas, hessian or tarpaulin covering. Rig up four uprights, far enough apart and tall enough to cover you if you sit on a stool between them. You may need cross-bars at the top to hold them firm.

Cover the frame with the cloth and tack it onto the wood, making sure that it is tight and will not flap about in the wind. One side needs to be free, a door with a hook for fastening it once you are inside. On another side you need a viewing flap or slot cut into the cloth, at the right height for your eyes when you are sitting down. You can take in a tripod and use a camera or a telescope. The hide must *not* be put close to a nest where it will scare away the birds.

Try a hide by a pool, instead, and watch birds coming to drink - or by a bird table. It is fun getting close views, even of everyday birds.

SPOTTER'S HINT
Try to use natural features of the landscape so that your hide is not too obvious - but do not cut down branches from trees to camouflage it.

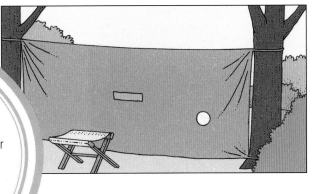

A SIMPLE HIDE
Set up a simple hide made from a piece of sacking or even an old fence panel, then you can watch birds at a drinking pool or at food put out to lure them to the spot.

WHICH BIRD IS IT?

Once you know what bird you are looking at, a new world of enjoyment opens up. You can read about what it eats, where it nests, if it migrates, and even learn new things that none of your friends know about it. First, though, you simply have to identify what it is.

IDENTIFICATION

Every kind of bird, or species, is different. They are as different from each other as cat, dog, sheep and cow. But some look very similar, and so identifying them is difficult, even for the experts. Others, such as mute swans, are easy.

Many species look different according to their age, sex and the time of year, too. For example, an old swan is white, but a young one is blotched with brown. An old herring gull is grey and white, a young one is blotched with brown, and a two-year-old is even mixed grey and white with brown spots! And that's not all: an adult herring gull in summer has a white head, whereas in winter it gets a streaky brown head. The point is that any bird will look very much like any other of the same kind, age and sex - which means you can check what they all are in a book.

FIELD NOTES

The best way to start is to learn the basic, common birds from an identification book, a field guide. If you see something you don't recognize, don't panic. Instead, study it carefully. First, consider its size and shape; then look at its bill and legs, and general colours. Next, look carefully at all parts of its plumage and note down what you see.

If you note things around a rough sketch, you will make sure you don't miss out something significant. It is best to make your notes in a spiral-bound notebook. Try to make them while you are watching the bird. You can then copy them up neatly at home.

WHAT IS THIS BIRD?

The bird you can see here has a round body, short and pointed wingtips, and a short tail. It also has a small, round head and longish legs. These show that it is a wader. The broad body but small, round head identify it as a plover. Because it has black legs, black, white and grey speckles all over its back, and a quite thick black bill, it is a grey plover.

If it flew, it would show white above the tail, and strange black 'armpit' patches, which would make it even easier to identify because nothing else has such a pattern.

SKETCHING BIRDS

When doing a field sketch, don't worry if it's not very life-like. Why not start with an egg-shape for the body and a smaller egg-shape for the head? Just add on the bill, legs, wings and tail. Then label each of the different parts with their colours.

Grey Plover *Pluvialis squatarola* L. 2... Breeding an...
Common winter visitor to coastal m... W Europe and NW Africa. Us... ...re... will search ... are...

Medium – large, silver-grey wader

Dark cap of thick, black streaks

Pale nape, dark ear coverts

White forehead and over eye

Darker black spots

Lighter black spots

Bill short but quite heavy, black

Dark wing tips

Legs black

White

Breastband of grey streaks between white chin and lower breast

Slow walk; stopped to tip forward while feeding

Big black 'armpit' patch

Called high thin 'tee-oo-ee' in flight

White on rump and tail

Thin white wing bar

Grey Plover

juv.

juv.

Golden Plover

Pacific Golden Plover

juv.

American Golden Plover

juv.

juv.

juv.

Dotterel

117

SPOTTER'S HINT
Always note the date, time, weather and exact place you see birds. There's no need to write down every one, just the most interesting, important and unusual.

25

FIELD GUIDES

It is important to be patient and careful when you use a field guide, and not jump to conclusions. Don't just find the first bird that looks a bit like the one in your pictures. Read the text about its plumage, calls and habits, too, and check the distribution maps - it would be a bit silly to identify a bird that should be thousands of kilometres away at that time of year!

A PRIVATE BIRD DIARY

When keeping a bird diary, you will want to do two things at once. First, you need to keep your notes in day order, so you can see where you've been and what you saw. It will also help to see the comings and goings at each place. If you keep a real diary, you will even see who you were with and what the weather was like - maybe even with photographs.

You might like to have your notes in species order. That means you can look up all your notes about a particular species instead of having to leaf through pages and pages of a day-to-day diary.

Why not keep a good daily diary *and* a separate card-index for the more interesting birds? You can store the cards in a simple box, arranged in the same order as the birds in your field guide.

Good records help you make better use of your birdwatching observations. A card index keeps things neat and tidy.

FIELD MARKS

Special marks on a bird are called field marks. They help identify what you see. Look for lines across the closed wing (and along the open wing in flight) - these are 'wingbars'. Stripes through the eyes are 'eyestripes'; ones over the eye, like eyebrows, are called 'superciliary stripes'. Many birds have white sides to the tail, or 'white outer tail feathers'. Others have streaks on the back, or spots on the breast, or patches of colour on the wing. The diagrams show some other field marks.

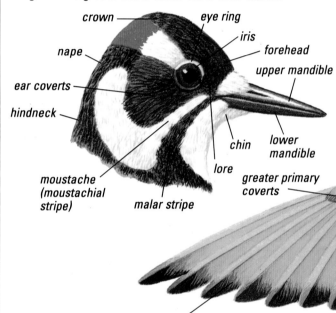

crown — eye ring
nape — iris
ear coverts — forehead
hindneck — upper mandible
moustache (moustachial stripe) — chin
malar stripe — lower mandible
lore — greater primary coverts
primaries

SPOTTER'S HINT
Study your notes to spot patterns of behaviour, or migration times, of each species. For example, at a lake you might find more waders when water levels are low, after a hot summer.

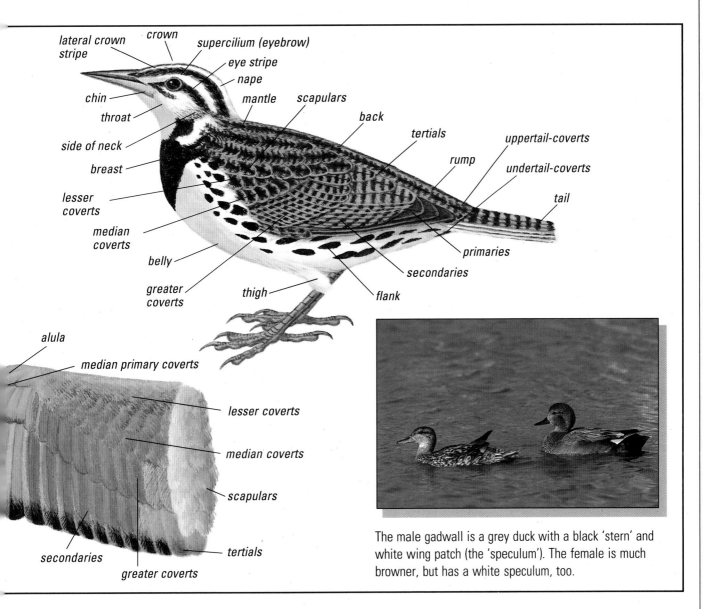

lateral crown stripe
crown
supercilium (eyebrow)
eye stripe
nape
chin
mantle
scapulars
throat
back
side of neck
tertials
uppertail-coverts
breast
rump
undertail-coverts
lesser coverts
tail
median coverts
belly
primaries
greater coverts
secondaries
thigh
flank

alula
median primary coverts
lesser coverts
median coverts
scapulars
secondaries
tertials
greater coverts

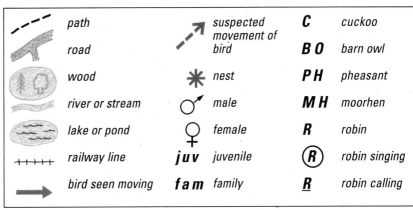

The male gadwall is a grey duck with a black 'stern' and white wing patch (the 'speculum'). The female is much browner, but has a white speculum, too.

MAPPING BIRD SIGHTINGS

Good maps are the basis for a breeding bird census, an official count of their numbers. Listening for their song is just as important as seeing the birds. Observers use standard symbols to represent what they have found so that anybody can understand their records. You, too, can use the selection of symbols and codes shown here when you are keeping notes.

- - -	path	
	road	
	wood	
	river or stream	
	lake or pond	
+++++	railway line	
→	bird seen moving	
↗	suspected movement of bird	
✳	nest	
♂	male	
♀	female	
juv	juvenile	
fam	family	

C	cuckoo
B O	barn owl
P H	pheasant
M H	moorhen
R	robin
Ⓡ	robin singing
<u>*R*</u>	robin calling

BETTER BIRD PHOTOGRAPHY

Taking pictures of birds is not too difficult. But taking *good* pictures of birds is very difficult indeed! Obviously, the way to become a good photographer is to practise, and to learn from your mistakes.

PRACTICE MAKES PERFECT

Whatever happens, it is good fun to try taking bird photographs, but don't expect great results right away. You have to be patient. You need plenty of time, and good equipment. And photography isn't a cheap hobby. A good camera is very expensive, and even film and printing are costly.

If you want to have a go, why not borrow a camera or consider some cheaper, secondhand ones before deciding what to buy? That way, you can see if you want to continue taking photographs, or would rather just go out and watch birds.

Having decided that bird photography really is for you, there's no need to rush out and buy the first camera you like the look of. It's worth comparing different models to find the most suitable for your needs - and it's important to choose a camera you can use comfortably.

Why not ask a dealer to take some test shots, so you can see what sort of results you'll get?

LOOKING THROUGH THE LENS

To do serious bird photography, you need a single-lens reflex (SLR) camera with changeable lenses. 'Single-lens reflex' means that a mirror reflects light coming into the lens, up through the eyepiece you look into. Thus you see exactly the picture that the camera will take.

With an SLR camera you can fit a range of telephoto lenses to magnify the bird more, making it look bigger in the picture.

A good bag keeps all your camera equipment dry and easy to find in a hurry.

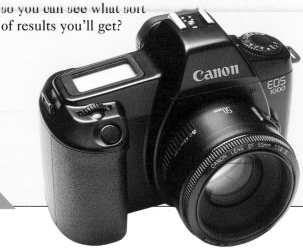

Cameras are expensive, but there's no point buying one that isn't up to the job. Get the best you can afford.

Try out several films and see which you like. They cost a lot, but it's not worth spoiling your efforts with poor material.

A tripod helps steady your camera, and is vital if you have a long lens.

BETTER BIRD PHOTOGRAPHY

If you have a hide you can use a 200mm or 300mm lens, which will give you a reasonable amount of magnification. Without a hide, you have to take pictures from farther away, so you may need longer lenses - maybe very powerful 400mm or 500mm ones. These are heavy and very expensive, but you can't do much longer-distance photography without them, except for pictures of flocks of birds.

A 50mm lens is of little use for small birds.

A 600mm lens makes birds look much bigger.

A good lens will make all the difference - a high-magnification one will give you the close-ups you want. Like all equipment, it should last a lifetime if you treat it carefully.

SPOTTER'S HINT
If you use a long lens, have the camera on a tripod, otherwise the lens will shake and wobble. Even the tiniest movement - one you can't even see - can blur the picture.

THE RIGHT FILM

You need 'slow' film for very good quality, but it is easier taking photos with 'fast' film. Fast film lets you use a faster shutter speed, which means you can 'freeze' the action of a bird. A slow shutter speed leaves a moving bird blurred in the picture. Fast film also lets you take pictures in duller light. But it also gives a coarser, grainy image. Bearing these points in mind, you need to use the slowest film you can in the conditions. Ideally it might be 64 ASA or 100 ASA, both slow films. If you use a faster 200 ASA film, the results may be okay, but 400 ASA or even 1000 ASA will probably give poorer results.

Professionals use colour transparency (slide) film. The pictures in this book were taken on slides. But you might like prints to show around, or stick in your bird diary - they are much easier to enjoy.

'Slow' film gives a sharper picture.

'Fast' film tends to give a grainy look.

CARE AND CONSIDERATION

Don't be tempted to take pictures of birds at a nest. It is difficult to do properly, and therefore a job for an expert. Remember, care for the birds must come first. That is the bird photographer's first rule. No-one should risk making a bird desert its eggs or young, not even for the best photograph. Besides, with some birds it is illegal to disturb them by the nest. The best place to take photos is near your garden feeder or a pond. Try a pool in a wood: but make sure there is some sunshine - deep inside a wood is too dark for good pictures.

TAKING TO THE AIR

Most birds fly, and many of them are masters of the air. The best can spend the great majority of their lives aloft. For example, the young swift may fly for three years before landing for the first time!

LIGHT AND AIRY

Birds' bones are super-strong but very light. They have hollow centres with a honeycomb structure, like aeroplanes and racing cars. This saves weight but makes them stiff, so they can support long feathers on long wings.

The feathers themselves are strong, too. The central shaft makes them stiff so that the big feathers on a bird's wing push powerfully against the air and move the bird along. As the bird moves forwards, so the shape of the wing, known as an aerofoil, makes the air go farther, and therefore faster, over the top than underneath. This means that there is less air pressure on top than underneath, so the bird is pushed upwards: it gains 'lift'.

EFFECTIVE MUSCLE

Big muscles attached to the breastbone of a bird pull the wings downwards. The heart is strong and beats very fast, the blood hot and full of oxygen from large, pumping lungs. This gives the bird an enormous amount of energy, helping it to get airborne and to move quickly over very long distances

SAILPLANES

Some birds have slight bodies, and long, narrow wings. They don't fly by beating their wings a lot, but by gliding. Albatrosses glide along on the air currents that rise off the slopes of ocean waves. Eagles soar on the wind that sweeps up above mountain cliffs. Vultures ride on 'bubbles' of hot air that form each morning in hot places over land. All of them glide without using up precious energy.

Birds of prey have 'fingers' at their wingtips where the edges of their feathers are cut away to make 'slots' between them. These reduce turbulence at the wingtip, making them extremely stable in the air. Aeroplanes have similar slots in their wings for the same reason.

The tail is used as a rudder to steer a bird in flight. A tern (left) or kite twists its forked tail to give extra agility.

Swans have to take off from water, running along the surface to get up enough speed for lift-off.

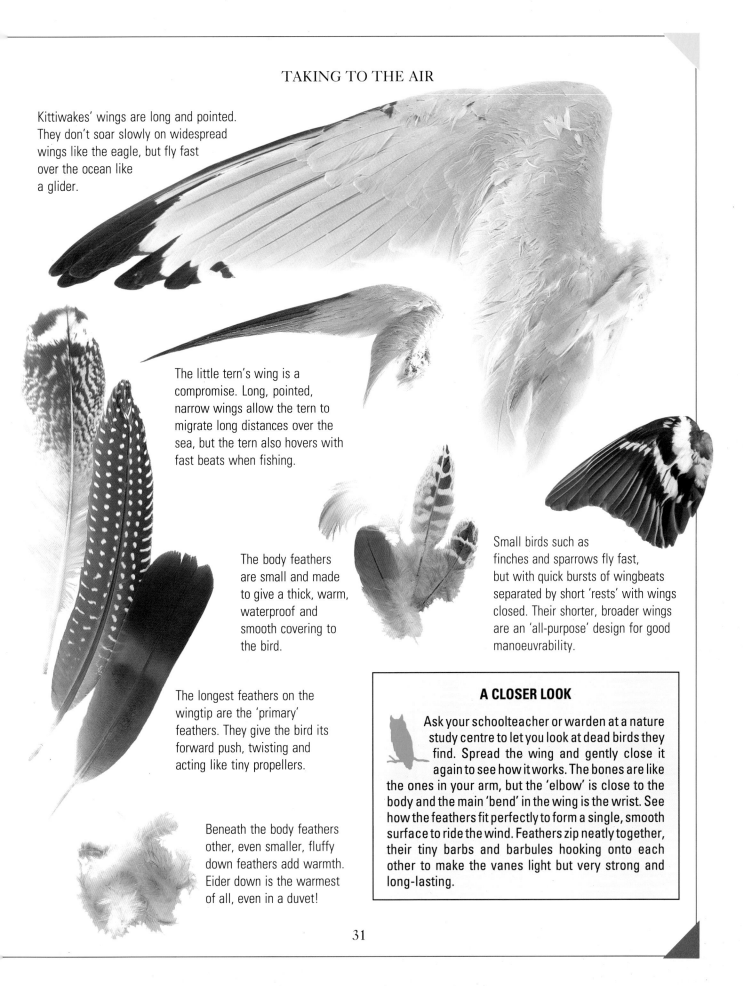

Kittiwakes' wings are long and pointed. They don't soar slowly on widespread wings like the eagle, but fly fast over the ocean like a glider.

The little tern's wing is a compromise. Long, pointed, narrow wings allow the tern to migrate long distances over the sea, but the tern also hovers with fast beats when fishing.

The body feathers are small and made to give a thick, warm, waterproof and smooth covering to the bird.

Small birds such as finches and sparrows fly fast, but with quick bursts of wingbeats separated by short 'rests' with wings closed. Their shorter, broader wings are an 'all-purpose' design for good manoeuvrability.

The longest feathers on the wingtip are the 'primary' feathers. They give the bird its forward push, twisting and acting like tiny propellers.

Beneath the body feathers other, even smaller, fluffy down feathers add warmth. Eider down is the warmest of all, even in a duvet!

A CLOSER LOOK

Ask your schoolteacher or warden at a nature study centre to let you look at dead birds they find. Spread the wing and gently close it again to see how it works. The bones are like the ones in your arm, but the 'elbow' is close to the body and the main 'bend' in the wing is the wrist. See how the feathers fit perfectly to form a single, smooth surface to ride the wind. Feathers zip neatly together, their tiny barbs and barbules hooking onto each other to make the vanes light but very strong and long-lasting.

PLUMES AND PATTERNS

Birds' feathers have many uses, including camouflage or attracting attention. And their shapes and colours help make birds so varied and exciting to look at.

Dull or patterned feathers can give a bird good camouflage, just like a soldier's patterned uniform. Not all camouflage has to be dull, though. It can break up a bird's outline, by being a mixture of strong colours, or patterns of black and white. If the bird keeps still, the pattern makes its shape hard to pick out. Masters of camouflage, such as the woodcock, are perfect mimics of dead leaves and grasses. They have beautiful and very detailed colour schemes. Bitterns have striped feathers and stand upright, so they look just like the reeds in which they live.

The ringed plover sits on its nest in stones and seashells. Its black and white pattern in the light and shade of the pebbles makes it invisible.

SHOWING OFF

Bright colours are used to attract attention instead of to hide. Male birds will often need to attract females, or to threaten other males. They do so with bright feathers, strong colours or strange shapes - the most famous example of a show-off of this kind is the peacock. Egrets have long, wispy, delicate plumes like the foliage of weeping willows. Ruffs have special ear tufts and colourful adornments on their necks. And even common pheasants have shiny, strikingly-patterned plumage and long tails.

CHANGING WITH AGE

Gulls are brown when they are young. They don't look like other, rival adult gulls, which are white, so they run less risk of being attacked by their own parents. When they get older they turn whiter, because they need to look different when they are old enough to fight for a territory and a mate. By watching herring gulls you can see how many of them are one year old, two years old, three years old or more. You can see the differences easily. On small birds, this is much harder to watch.

1st winter

2nd winter

3rd winter

adult
breeding

adult winter

juvenile

adult
breeding

Mediterranean
sub-species

Seabirds such as the sooty tern are dark on top, so they are not easily seen from above by predators. But they are white underneath and along the front of their wings and forehead. That makes them hard to see from underwater against the sky and when they are diving. That way they get closer to fish.

By looking at the amount of purple and blue in its feathering, you can tell whether an indigo bunting is a male or female, and even roughly how old it is: the bluest are old males.

MOULT

Birds' feathers last only about a year. They need replacing, in a regular process called moult, which often takes place before migration. Each feather loosens and falls out, and is replaced by a new one.

Of course, they don't all fall out at once or the bird would die. So each bird has a regular pattern, with the larger feathers falling out in the same order, at the same time of year, one by one. Wing feathers take the longest time to be changed, as most birds want to fly during moult. Several bird families, including ducks, geese, swans, divers and grebes, lose all their flight feathers at once and can't fly for a while.

Kingfishers have shiny feathers, their colours being made up of special reflections from the actual structure of the feather. Most other birds have 'pigments', like dyes, in their feathers, which give them their colours.

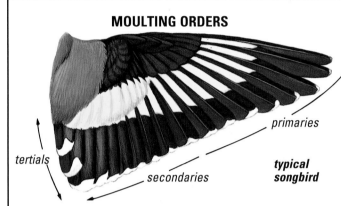

MOULTING ORDERS

primaries

tertials

secondaries

typical songbird

Birds' feathers are replaced in a regular sequence. This is always the same for particular species. Most songbirds start from the innermost primary, working out, and from the outermost secondary inwards.

For a short time each summer, the male mallard loses his striking plumage, and looks much more like the female.

COLOURS ECLIPSED

Male mallards are usually bright and gaudy. They display to each other and show off to the females. The females are dull and brown. It is these that have to sit tight on the eggs for several weeks until they hatch. They have to be well hidden.

In late summer, male ducks have a duller, darker plumage for a few weeks, coinciding with their moult. This is called 'eclipse'. It is really the duck's non-breeding plumage, because courtship and mating take place during the winter and spring.

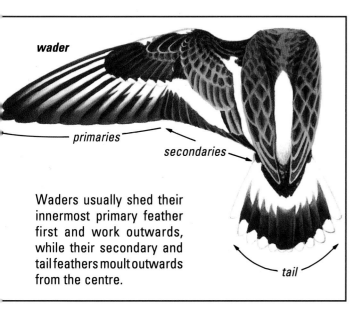

wader

primaries

secondaries

Waders usually shed their innermost primary feather first and work outwards, while their secondary and tail feathers moult outwards from the centre.

tail

CHANGING WITH THE SEASONS

During moult, changes in colour are gradual, because feathers are never replaced all at one time. A good example of a bird which makes a gradual seasonal change is the ptarmigan. The ptarmigan turns white in winter, when it lives in deep snow. In spring it is patchy white and grey. By summer, after the snow has melted, it has changed to brown to match the colour of the speckled rocks and lichens.

Chaffinches have brown heads in the winter. In spring, the pale brown tips of the feathers suddenly break up and fall away. Underneath they reveal clean, bright blue-grey. The chaffinch changes colour without changing any feathers!

Snowy owls are white, and they hide away in the snow. But they aren't hiding from predators, as ptarmigans do, but are keeping out of sight of their prey. They are using their camouflage for hunting, not for defence.

Wheatears have plumages that look eyecatching in a book. But on the rocky slope of a mountain, the black, white and grey colours are lost against the background, helping to protect the birds from keen-eyed predators.

DISPLAY AND SONGFLIGHT

Display is just showing off. It is used by male birds to attract females (like boys posing at a disco). And it is used to avoid real fighting, by birds that need to defend their living space from intruders (like boys threatening but not hitting each other).

COURTSHIP

Trying to find a mate and establish a relationship is the main reason for many displays and songs. Some birds pair with the same mates for the whole of their lives, most for just one summer. Others don't stay together at all, and it is these, where one male mates with all the females and then scoots off, that often have strange displays. Typical of the one-season pairs are starlings. Males sing and wave their wings in order to attract a female. When she shows an interest, he sings and waves his wings all the more, and leads her to a likely place to nest. You can easily see the song and display in spring.

The grouse family includes real show-offs, like male capercaillies, black grouse, ruffed grouse and prairie chickens. Males get together to display, using their colours, strangely-shaped feathers and special sounds. Females watch and choose the best-looking or most aggressive male. That way, their chicks should be strongest and most likely to survive.

Moorhens fight to get a mate and territory. Their noisy battles are often seen in the spring. They kick with their feet and splash with their rounded wings.

Ruffs display, or 'lek', at a special place called a 'hill'. Males have mock fights and the females creep up to see what's going on. They choose the strongest males, which defend the centre of the hill, to mate with. Sometimes some males on the fringe mate, too.

GRACE AND POWER

Grebes display every spring but may stay together for life. They need to be sure of each other during many weeks of looking after eggs and chicks. They need a pair-bond to keep them together, and strengthen it by special, elaborate displays using colourful head-plumes in graceful 'dances' on the water.

In contrast, bald eagles and golden eagles display to their mates by showing off their skill in the air, swooping up and down in great rollercoaster rides across the sky and diving in 160 km/hr stoops. These also tell other eagles 'keep away - this piece of territory is mine'.

Great crested grebes have elegant spring displays. They face each other and wag their heads, swim side-by-side and dive together, touch their backs with their beaks, and offer each other bits of weed.

TROPICAL SPLENDOUR

In the tropics, displays are taken to extremes. Birds of paradise have magnificent plumes that are used in special courtship extravaganzas. Bowerbirds build special structures and decorate them with colourful berries, leaves and even bits of glass, wool or plastic. Then they display inside them. The quetzals of the Central American forests have long, whippy tail feathers, and look like 'flying snakes' when they make their magnificent courtship flights.

The birds of paradise of New Guinea, such as this Raggiana bird of paradise, are famous for their displays of their brilliant plumage.

If their display song doesn't deter intruders, European robins are fierce in defending their territories. Some males may even kill other robins in spring.

Puffins fight over the ownership of a nesting burrow. They grasp each other's bills and strike out with their feet, which have needle-sharp claws. Sometimes they roll way down steep slopes and fall over cliffs.

DRUMMING AND BOOMING

Snipe use a different way of showing that they are claiming a territory to nest in. They fly high in the air, then spread out special, stiff tail feathers and dive steeply in a series of switchback swoops. The tail feathers vibrate and make a loud humming noise with each dive. This is called 'drumming'.

Another kind of drumming is used by woodpeckers. They find a good, hard branch that makes a loud, echoing sound when hit hard. Then they rain a stream of blows with the bill onto the wood, in a sudden, short, noisy burst of sound that carries through the forest.

Bitterns live in dense reedbeds and could have a problem finding mates - you can't see far in a reedbed! So they make remarkable, deep, booming sounds which carry several kilometres.

All of these special sounds are used in the way that other birds use their songs.

SONGS

In general, visual displays are more common in open habitats, whereas song is used to advertise a bird's presence where visibility is limited.

Bird songs and calls are used to convey messages. It is those which are used as a form of display while establishing a territory and attracting a mate that are often the most beautiful. Some of the best songsters are the thrushes and warblers: if you can't identify any of the very similar-looking warblers by sight, try listening to their songs!

SONGFLIGHTS

Many small birds of open habitats fly up and sing over their territories, performing distinctive songflights.

However, when they fly into the air they are taking the risk of being seen more easily by predators.

 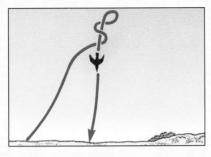 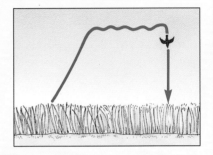

The male bobolink of North America has no perches to sing from in open grassy country. Instead, he flies up and hovers, starts his bubbling song, then descends in a quivering, fluttery flight while getting carried away with his ecstatic singing.

Skylarks sing in high, hovering flights over open spaces where there are no decent perches to sing from. They can keep up their continuous and excited song for half an hour or more. After their song, they plummet to the ground and land silently.

Sedge warblers and whitethroats sing from bushes, but every so often they will fly up a short way in a steep, fluttery flight. They descend to another bush nearby, singing as they do so. Reed warblers and lesser whitethroats never do this.

Its stiff outer tail feathers tremble in the rush of air as a snipe dives, making a loud humming noise.

Bitterns are heard but not seen - their booming calls carry 2-3 km through the dense reeds they live in.

A VOICE IN THE AIR

Bird songs and calls are often very beautiful, while others can be more tiresome! Whether or not they are attractive, they are very useful to the birdwatcher. Not only do they let you find the bird more easily than by sight alone - you can hear a bird in a dense tree where you can never see it - but they can usually identify it, too.

THE SOUND OF BIRDS

You need to learn the bird sounds, of course. The simplest way is to listen to common birds that you can see, and note the sounds they make: a 'chirrup' call of a house sparrow, or 'tick' of a wren, for example. Many field guides explain some calls and songs, too. With these, you may need to go out and listen to some common birds to find out how the book has interpreted the calls. But to learn many of the less common songs and calls, the best way is to listen to professional recordings on cassettes.

If you want to hear bird song and the sounds of tropical forests or remote lakes, the very best recordings come on compact discs. The clarity and atmosphere are wonderful.

YOUR OWN RECORDINGS

Even with a small tape recorder and microphone, you too can make quite good recordings of birds. Go out with a few cassettes of tape and see what you can get - unlike photographic film, tape can be used again. It is best to set the recorder to 'record', with the 'pause' button on, then stop the 'pause' when you want to record - that way there are no 'clicks'.

Wind on the microphone is often a problem. And you will be amazed how even a one-directional microphone picks up the noise of distant traffic, barking dogs, or people talking next door. Be patient, because it takes a lot of practice and experience to get really good results.

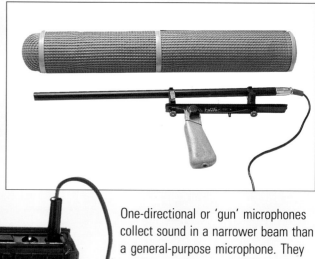

One-directional or 'gun' microphones collect sound in a narrower beam than a general-purpose microphone. They can be mounted on a handle. The cover (shown detached) helps to filter out some of the background noise.

A good and sturdy cassette tape recorder is used by professionals to get high-quality recordings. If you are going to walk with a recorder, a shoulder strap is vital to leave your hands free for holding the microphone and working the recording buttons. Headphones let you listen to the recordings as you go along.

40

Try placing a microphone on a stand in a sheltered spot, maybe near a bird feeder or a roost site. Use a very long lead and sit back in a hide or sheltered inside the house with your recorder. You may be able to use earphones to hear what you are recording. That way, you can stay out of sight and leave the birds undisturbed, while you record their calls.

FOR THE RECORD

Unfortunately, it is not so easy to keep your best recordings, unless you have a tape-to-tape recorder at home, and can edit them. Be sure to label them properly, because sounds with no references are useless. You should write down the name of the bird, what it was doing, when and where.

REFLECTORS

For the serious enthusiast, a parabolic reflector is worth buying. It is a big, round dish, a bit like a television satellite dish, with a microphone mounted in the centre. The microphone collects sounds reflected from the dish and you record a magnified sound from a narrow source. You can focus on an individual bird and also keep out some of the background noises, including other birds.

MAKING A PARABOLIC REFLECTOR

How about trying an old umbrella as a dish? A lining of baking foil or metallic silver paint will increase its reflecting properties. You will need to make some test recordings with the microphone in different positions on the handle, to find the focus of the sound. It will probably need to be fixed about 15-20 centimetres from the hood.

It is usually best to get up and go out very early. Birds, such as this male blackbird, sing best then, and there are fewer noises that you don't want to record. But don't just go for the dawn chorus; the most spectacular sounds can be from winter flocks of geese, waders and cranes.

SPOTTER'S HINT
If you don't have a parabolic reflector, you can tape your microphone to a stick so that it won't pick up the rustle of your hands.

FUTURE GENERATIONS

Most people die in their relatively old age. But most birds usually don't get a chance to live that long. Because modern medicine is so good in western countries, most people need just two children to make sure that the total population stays the same when they eventually die. Birds and most other wild creatures need to rear far more than that. The reason is that most young birds die within a few months. To get two to survive to replace their parents, maybe several dozen need to be reared over a few years.

DICING WITH DEATH

Birds are nearly always in danger. Very many are killed by hawks and foxes. In the United Kingdom, cats and cars each kill another 70 million birds a year. And others die of disease, starvation and cold. Yet most species are very stable - there are roughly the same number of thrushes, kestrels, and so on, year after year. This is because they maintain a balance with their environment. The number of eggs they lay and young they rear, and the number of young that survive to breeding age themselves, just match the numbers needed to replace the adult birds as they die. If they didn't, the population would go up and down in a chaotic series of changes.

There are several ways in which the numbers are kept so well balanced. Birds have different ways of rearing young, and each works well for the kind of life they lead. A lot depends on the food that they can find. Feeding themselves is hard enough for a pair of adult birds. Suddenly having new mouths to feed, with a family of growing chicks, is extra hard work. Only if they have timed their nesting just right will they be able to do it.

Big birds such as golden and American bald eagles have few enemies. They also live longer than smaller songbirds. That means that they may have 10 years to rear just two young. They usually lay just two eggs a year and rear only one chick. Most chicks die quite soon, often in their first winter of trying to fend for themselves. But eventually one or two of them will make it - just enough to keep the population going.

Wild geese, swans and cranes feed in flocks in the winter but family groups stay together within the larger gatherings. It is easy to count how many young have been reared by each pair each year and how many pairs have failed.

RAISING A BROOD

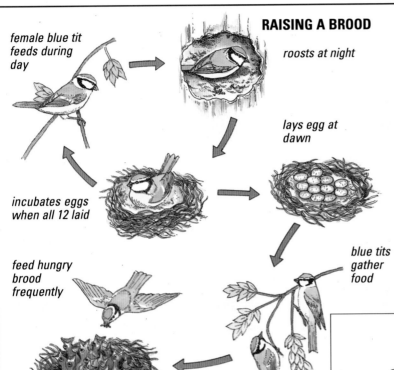

female blue tit feeds during day

roosts at night

lays egg at dawn

incubates eggs when all 12 laid

feed hungry brood frequently

blue tits gather food

Blue tits really put all their eggs in one basket. They rear just one brood of young each year. They lay about 10 or 12 eggs. The birds pair up, build a nest and lay their eggs. They then incubate them (sit on them to keep them warm) until they hatch at precisely the time when millions of tiny green caterpillars are hatching all over the fresh leaves of late spring. Suddenly, the blue tits have never seen so much food. They can take 800 caterpillars to their hungry chicks every day. A week too soon, or a week too late, and the food would not be there. But, if they time it right, they can easily feed a dozen babies.

Blackbirds do things differently from blue tits. They feed their chicks on worms. A few worms they can always get - but never hundreds at a time! They couldn't possibly find enough to feed 12 chicks at once. Instead, they have four at a time, but rear three families during the summer. In the end, although they have taken months to do it, they still rear 12 chicks like the blue tits.

three clutches

spring *summer* *autumn*

A NATURAL BALANCE

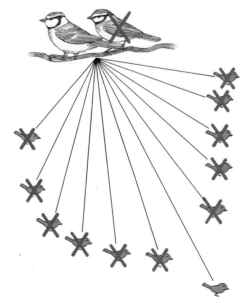

If 12 baby blue tits and both parents survived until next spring, there would be 14 birds where a year ago there were just two. It can't happen. Instead, 12 of the 14 die. That is why there are so many birds for sparrowhawks, kestrels, magpies, cats, weasels and other predators to eat. If only 11 die instead of 12, the population could increase by half! Instead, the numbers will balance out over a large area and the total will stay about the same.

NESTS

Nests are not 'homes' for birds. They are simply the places where they lay their eggs. The eggs are kept warm - incubated - until they hatch. Then the chicks may stay in the nest for a time, or leave right away.

The chick develops inside the egg, where it is kept at just the right temperature. Parent birds sit on the eggs to keep them warm. They have bare 'brood patches' on their bodies, where the feathers fall from a patch of skin full of hot blood vessels.

When the chick is old enough, it may 'talk' to its parent from inside the egg, before it hatches. It uses a special 'egg tooth' on the tip of its bill to break its way out of the hard shell.

EGGS

Eggs are very variable. Those laid in dark holes by owls, kingfishers and woodpeckers are white to make them easier to see. Those on pebbly beaches, such as tern and plover eggs, are spotted brown and sandy colour, for camouflage.

(not to scale)

guillemot

golden plover

little tern

nightjar

EGGS

In the UK and other parts of the world, birds' eggs are protected by law, just like the birds. It is illegal to collect them. Anyway, it is a silly thing to do. Eggs are much better left to hatch into new young birds. Stealing the eggs of very rare birds is particularly serious, and can cause the birds to die out. And egg-thieves face fines of up to £1,000 *for each egg.*

The reed warbler builds a nest in vertical reeds. It fastens the deep cup-shaped nest to several growing reed stems.

Ravens make nests of big, heavy sticks, placed under overhangs on sheer cliffs, well out of any predator's reach.

Woodpeckers dig their own nests out of the trunks of trees, chipping out the wood with their chisel bills.

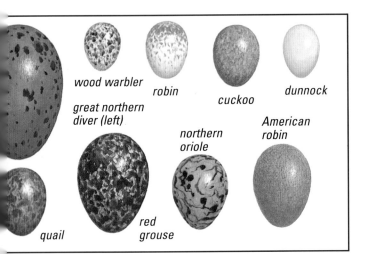

wood warbler

robin

cuckoo

dunnock

great northern
diver (left)

northern
oriole

American
robin

quail

red
grouse

JUVENILE AND IMMATURE

In bird books, young birds are often described by the terms juvenile and immature. 'Juvenile' means a bird that is still in its very first set of feathers, those that it had when it left the nest. These are usually changed by the autumn. 'Immature' is a bird that is not yet old enough to breed - with bigger species and seabirds, it may be three or four years, or even more, before a bird has grown up to be an adult.

YOUNG BIRDS

Helpless, naked, blind chicks need to be kept warm and sheltered. They take a long time to grow feathers and to get big enough to move off. Typical garden birds and songbirds are like this.

Baby ducklings are fluffy and active as soon as they hatch. They leave the nest and even feed themselves the day they are born. They may seem easy prey, but they can swim and dive; and they don't risk staying in a nest that a fox might find.

Owls incubate their eggs once the first is laid, so some of the chicks hatch a week before the others. These are bigger and quick to grab food. If there's enough, the smaller chicks get fed; if not, they starve, and the bigger ones survive - which is better than all of them starving.

INJURED AND LOST BIRDS

If you see a baby bird calling to be fed and you think it is lost, LEAVE IT ALONE. It almost certainly isn't lost. When you go away its parents will come to feed it, so leave the area quickly. Whatever you do, never pick up a baby bird and take it home.

Injured birds are extremely difficult to care for. If you find one, keep it warm in an airy box, then call for expert help - probably from a local vet. Be prepared that most injured birds are likely to be put to sleep, as there is little we can do for many of them. Those that can recover need constant care and attention.

Many species of cuckoo lay their eggs in other birds' nests. The female watches other birds until she finds a nest with fresh eggs. Then she takes one egg, lays one of her own, and leaves. The cuckoo egg hatches out very quickly and the baby cuckoo kills the other nestlings, so that it gets all the food from its foster parents, such as this dunnock.

BEAKS AND FEET

A bird's beak, or bill, is crucial to its survival. It uses it to grab and handle its food. It cleans its feathers with it like a comb. It builds its nest with it. It may fight with it, or dig holes with it. The bill has to be just right for the bird's way of life and the kind of place where it lives. You can learn a lot about a bird by looking at its bill. Its feet give good clues, too. This is why beaks and feet are so useful when it comes to identifying birds.

BEAKS AND BILLS

Waders such as dowitchers, snipe and godwits have long, slender bills that are used as probes in soft mud. The tip of the bill is sensitive enough to feel for worms. Once it finds one, the bill is flexible, and can open up underground and close tight on the worm.

Birds of prey have hooked bills for tearing meat. Bald eagles rip open salmon; golden eagles open up the hide of dead sheep and hares. A falcon's bill has a small 'notch' behind the hook so it can break the neck of birds or small mammals.

The very different spoonbill has a flattened beak that broadens into a disc at the tip. It holds it slightly open in shallow water and sweeps it from side to side. If it feels a fish, it snaps shut on its prey. Avocets do the same thing, but eat tiny shrimps and worms in very soft, wet mud or water. They have thin, up-turned bills that sweep sideways.

hawfinch　　　　　*grosbeak*

The hawfinch and grosbeak have bills that are designed for cracking hard seeds. They have short, deep, triangular beaks with sharp cutting edges and powerful plates inside for crushing seeds. Their cheeks bulge with strong muscle for working the bill around a cherry stone or a nut. Seeds are 'peeled' by rolling them against the edge of the bill with the tongue.

CRUSHING AND CATCHING

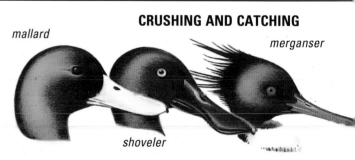

mallard　　　　　*merganser*

shoveler

Ducks have fascinating bills. Look at a mallard or shoveler on the park lake. Its bill is broad and quite flat. Inside it is like a sieve, and it can filter tiny seeds from mud and water. But mergansers have long, narrow bills with tiny hooks and serrated edges like saws. These are for gripping strong, slippery fish.

American bald eagles' feet are powerful killing tools. They have strong muscles and long, curved claws with sharp points. The front claws hold the prey with a crushing grip, while the hind claw stabs it like a dagger.

LEGS AND TOES

Snipe have quite short legs but long toes for walking on mud, and very long bills for probing for their food.

In contrast, stilts have very long legs for going into deep water, but shorter bills for picking insects from the water's surface.

A woodpecker's foot has two toes forward and two back (most birds have three forward, one back). The outer toe is long and can be swung sideways to get a grip around a narrow branch.

The pipit has a very long claw on its back toe, to help it balance and walk through long grass. Most song-birds have short toes and claws, and they move in short hops.

nighthawk   *nightjar*

The American nighthawks and European nightjars have tiny bills, like swifts'. But all of these birds have huge mouths! They catch insects in flight in mid air. Their mouths are wide and open up to snatch an insect, but the bill is almost useless. On nightjars there is a line of stiff hairs around the mouth that helps guide in the insects.

SPOTTER'S HINT
When it has been raining or snowing, keep an eye out for footprints. You'll know then where birds have been gathering. But it's difficult to identify what they were!

EATING TO SURVIVE

The main aim of most birds, most of the time, is to find food. Small birds, especially in the cold, short days of winter, spend nearly all day searching for food. Only rarely do they have an easy life. Larger birds survive longer on fewer, bigger meals. Big birds of prey need only one meal a day and can go several days without feeding if they have to. So they spend more time resting, just sitting about doing very little. They are not the all-action birds that we imagine them to be. Gulls and ducks also spend many hours seeming to do nothing. But watch flocks of tits, goldcrests and warblers and you will see them feeding non-stop, especially if they have young to care for. They are the real action birds.

FINDING FOOD

There are many ways of finding food and making the best of it. It all depends on the kind of food and the habitat. Some birds are loners, because their food is never very abundant, even though it may be widespread. Many of the thrushes are like that. If they eat worms or snails, there are rarely enough to feed whole flocks of them at once. Each needs some space to move around in, searching for scattered prey.

In contrast, seed-eaters, such as goldfinches and sparrows, can often find a lot of food in a small area. Therefore they may feed together and there is still enough to go round. So they live and feed and even nest in larger groups.

LOOSE FLOCKS

Some birds, such as godwits on a beach, seem to be better at finding food if they are in a scattered, loose flock than when they are alone. They find more worms and lose less to thieving gulls when they are in a group. But too many and they begin to fight each other for food and the advantage is lost. They need to be in a scattered flock, but not a dense one.

FINDING A NICHE

Some birds eat special types of food, while others are less choosy. If two kinds eat the same food, they will 'compete' - often one drives the other away. But if they eat different food, even two similar species may get along together, side-by side. They can also get along if they eat the same food but there is more than enough for both of them. Some birds of prey live happily together in

golden eagle 4,000g

buzzard 800g

sparrowhawk (female) (E) 260g

American kestrel (A) 200g

hare 4,000g

rabbit 500g

blackbird 100g

beetle 5g

one area because they take different prey. But hawks, such as sharp-shinned hawks and goshawks, all eat birds. They avoid competition for food by taking different sizes of bird and by being different sizes them-selves - even females are bigger than their mates. For example, male sparrowhawks take sparrows and tits, while the larger females go for thrushes and pigeons.

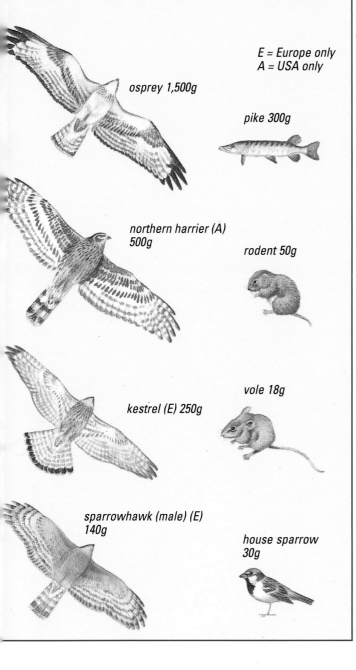

E = Europe only
A = USA only

osprey 1,500g

pike 300g

northern harrier (A) 500g

rodent 50g

kestrel (E) 250g

vole 18g

sparrowhawk (male) (E) 140g

house sparrow 30g

IN AMONGST THE CROWD

Other shorebirds, such as grey plovers, have feeding territories on the beach. Some of the best feeding places may be uncovered only briefly at low tide and sometimes may not be exposed at all. So the best place for a grey plover might be where there is a little less food, but where it is guaranteed to be available every day, or for longer. If too many grey plovers gather there, they spend too much time squabbling. They do better feeding instead of fighting.

Shrikes, such as this great grey shrike, catch big crunchy beetles, lizards, small voles and small birds by watching for them from a perch. They often spike them on a thorn to help tear them into pieces small enough to swallow.

FOOD PIRACY

Arctic skuas can catch fish, but find that it is usually easier to wait for puffins, kittiwakes and terns to catch them instead. Then they chase these other birds until they are so scared they drop the fish. The ferocious skuas will then snatch it up even before it drops to the sea. They are typical food pirates. Skuas also eat small birds and mammals, the great skua, for example, preying on penguins' eggs and chicks.

PROTECTING THEIR FOOD

Knots migrate vast distances. And to fly from the southern end of Africa or South America to the Arctic each year takes a lot of energy. So they have to have guaranteed food along the way. Therefore the river estuaries are absolutely vital to them. If we fill in and build on many more, the shorebirds are going to be in real trouble. As it is, knots move north in America and reach special bays just at the time that millions of horseshoe crabs are coming ashore to spawn there. There are millions of spare crab eggs. The knots have a feast, eating as much as they can, and there are still enough eggs to keep the crabs going. If the bays were to be polluted by an oil spill, or turned into an industrial site, the knots would face disaster.

These shorebirds (knots, with a few dunlins) rely on estuaries for most of their lives. Without the mudflats, which teem with millions of tiny creatures, they would not be able to feed during their globe-trotting travels or during the months when they have to leave the Arctic.

STAYING PUT OR MOVING ON

Owls can stay in one small area all their lives, or move around to find the best hunting. Some, like tawnies and great horned owls, stay in one place and learn every inch of it. They can live there successfully even in bad years, when food is scarce. But long-eared and snowy owls shift from place to place. They never get to know their territories very well, but it doesn't matter because they just move to new places with plenty of food. Either way works.

OWL PELLETS

Can you find a place where an owl or bird of prey roosts? Maybe you can collect some pellets. These are all the bits of prey that can't be digested, and are coughed back up through the mouth. If you tease them apart in a dish or plastic tub of water, you can pick out bones, feathers, bits of beetles and so on. You can see just what the bird has had for dinner!

Clean the bones and teeth you find with a tweezer and dry them with tissue. You can try to find what parts of the body they came from.

WAYS OF FEEDING

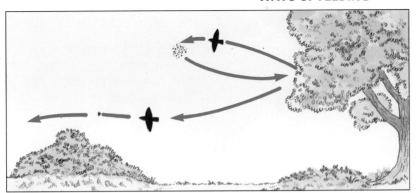

Flycatchers swoop out from a perch to take flies in mid air. Do you think they prefer clearings or woodland edges to dense trees? See if you can work out whether or not they are catching insects that fly over sunny spaces and show up against a dark background.

While great tits feed on and around big branches, blue tits get on to smaller twigs, and the tiny coal tits can move out to the very tip of the thinnest sprig. That way they can feed in a mixed flock but don't all go for the same food.

The slender, pointed bill of the goldfinch is made for picking seeds from deep inside thistles and teasels.

SPOTTER'S HINT
Early spring migrants find the insects they need few and far between. Very often you find the birds over or beside lakes and reservoirs, where there are more tiny flies to eat.

Shelducks find a good nest burrow and defend a territory around it, keeping other shelducks off. At the same time, the male finds a good feeding territory on the beach, and stakes a claim to that, too. When the chicks hatch, they are led across the dunes to the beach, to the feeding area already reserved for them.

FLOCKS

Some birds are never seen more than a few at a time - perhaps a family group at most - while others form large gatherings known as flocks. There are several reasons for flocking, and also for staying in ones and twos. If a bird feeds on food that is widely spread but never very abundant there would not be food for more than one or two at a time. But where food is plentiful, there is no reason why hundreds of birds should not feed together.

Spectacular flocks of oystercatchers flash black and white as they take off, dazzling predators, such as peregrines, which find it difficult to concentrate on one and may miss the lot!

SAFETY IN NUMBERS

A bird on its own might escape being seen by a predator. But if it is seen, it is the only choice the predator has. A flock gives a better chance of a predator being spotted - many eyes are better than two - and, if the predator comes close, there's a good chance it will kill one of the others anyway! So most birds in open spaces do well to keep in flocks when there are foxes, falcons or hawks about.

FINDING FOOD

Flocks also make it easier to find food. A bird on its own may find very little, but in a flock one bird is sure to find something - then all the rest can join in.

Shorebirds on a muddy estuary may feed in dense flocks and find food more efficiently than if they were widely spaced. This is because they can spend more time eating and less time looking out for hawks. Others, because they are eating worms which sink into the mud when disturbed, are more likely to catch worms on their own, without the noise of too many pattering feet. But even they have to form flocks when the tide comes in and they have to rest in some sheltered, safe place.

Cattle egrets feed in small groups in fields and dryer marshland, often alongside cattle. They flock together to roost in the few safe places.

EVENING ROOSTS

Even birds that feed in small groups may join up in larger flocks to spend the night. This may be because they need a safe place to sleep, like gulls on a lake or starlings in a reedbed, but it also helps those that have found little food to follow better-fed birds to good feeding areas the next morning. In roosting flocks the older, stronger birds sleep in the centre where it is warm and safest from predators, leaving younger, inferior birds out in the cold.

WATCHING FLOCKS

Look for flocks and note down the numbers of birds you see. Are the flocks of one species, two, or many? Some shorebirds and ducks stay separate, others intermingle. Starling flocks have no other birds mixed in, but thrush flocks can be of two or three species together.

It is also interesting studying the behaviour of whole flocks, rather than the birds within them. For example, do winter plover flocks select the same fields year after year? Or do they go for the same crops? Are they feeding on open spaces with no hedges, or close up to hedgerows and trees? Do gulls steal their food? If so, do you find that the less experienced young plovers lose more food to the gulls than adults?

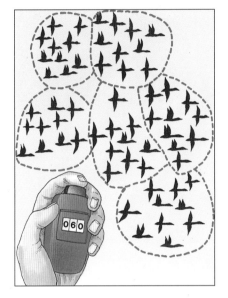

Small flocks can be easily counted one-by-one. But bigger groups need a quicker method - count up 10 birds, then divide the flock into tens, or even hundreds, and add up the groups.

Flocks of black-headed gulls follow the farm plough because huge numbers of worms and grubs are turned up - there's plenty of food for all.

ON THE LOOKOUT

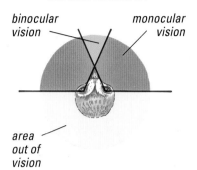

binocular vision   monocular vision

area out of vision

Birds of prey have magnificent eyes. They don't see things any larger than we do, but they see better detail. Birds of prey also have binocular vision, their eyes facing forward so that they can concentrate on their prey.

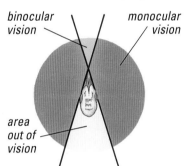

binocular vision   monocular vision

area out of vision

Other birds have their eyes set on the sides of their heads. This gives them a wider field of view, to spot predators.

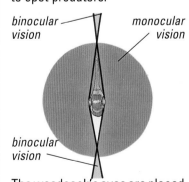

binocular vision   monocular vision

binocular vision

The woodcock's eyes are placed so that it can see completely around itself.

MIGRATION

Birds can move huge distances and even cross oceans. This means that many of them can migrate - they live in one area in one season of the year, and move elsewhere for another season. They migrate to avoid bad winter weather, or to find new supplies of food.

For example, many birds find the warm northern summers, with long, hot days and abundant insects, an irresistible attraction. Warblers are an example. They fatten up before they leave on their long non-stop flights. Most migrate at night, and navigate by the moon and stars. Swallows migrate by day. They use the sun as a guide, and eat insects as they go.

When these birds move south for the winter, thrushes and waxwings - even some woodpeckers, birds of prey and owls - move into the area left by the warblers. They come from even farther north, or escape the cold winters in the middle of northern continents by flying to the milder coastal regions.

NORTHERN VISITORS

Shorebirds breed on northern tundra. The summer there is very short, but daylight lasts for almost 24 hours a day. However, by autumn it becomes cold and dark and the birds have to go south. They don't return until late spring, after the snow begins to melt.

A DANGEROUS JOURNEY

Migration is difficult because it exhausts small birds and they face great danger, crossing mountains, seas and deserts. Lighthouse beams and lights on oil rigs at sea confuse migrating birds, many of which dash themselves to death against the dazzling lights.

Birds are carefully trapped by scientists so that numbered rings (bands) can be put on their legs. If the bird is later found dead or trapped again, the tiny label shows from where it has travelled and how long it has lived.

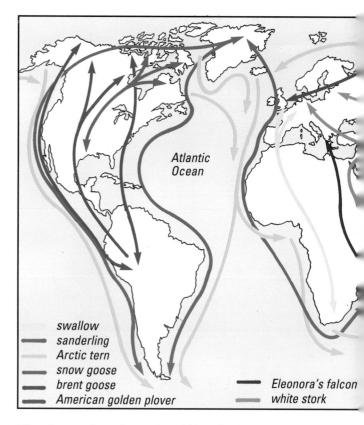

swallow
sanderling
Arctic tern
snow goose
brent goose
American golden plover
Eleonora's falcon
white stork

Migrating swallows fly south to Africa. Sanderlings and Arctic terns fly right across the globe, whereas brent and snow geese stay in the northern hemisphere. American golden plovers are among the fastest migrants; in contrast,

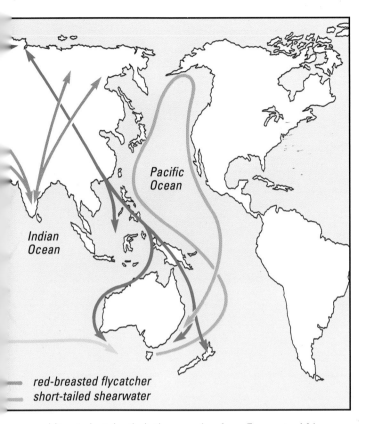

white storks take their time soaring from Europe to Africa. Eleonora's falcons eat small migrants. Seabirds such as the short-tailed shearwater travel the oceans worldwide. Red-breasted flycatchers fly to India from all across Asia.

red-breasted flycatcher
short-tailed shearwater

Waxwings (and, in North America, cedar waxwings) eat insects in summer but turn to fleshy berries in winter. They eat more than their own body weight in a day, and need plenty of water to drink, too.

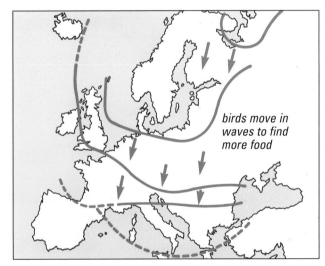

birds move in waves to find more food

Shorebirds need to feed in rich estuary mud. There are not many suitable estuaries; the best act as migration 'service stations' for millions of birds on their globetrotting travels. Without the estuaries - many of which are under threat from urban and industrial development - the birds would die.

If birds such as waxwings have had two or three successful breeding seasons, their numbers will be very high. If the berry crop is then very poor, large flocks of birds will fly great distances in search of new sources of food. This is called an 'eruption' from their normal range.

SPRING MIGRATION

Migration time is exciting for the birdwatcher. In spring, birds are eager to get to their breeding areas and claim a territory. Once the weather is good, they move quickly. If you want to see migrating waders or terns at a local lake, you will have to go as often as possible, because they will not be there for long. A migrant may pause for only an hour or so to rest and feed, before continuing on its way.

Excited by the prospect of good birdwatching, people gather at special migration watch points to see the show. Migrating hawks at Hawk Mountain, Pennsylvania, storks at Gibraltar, or incoming migrants along the coast of the English channel, all attract enthusiasts in autumn.

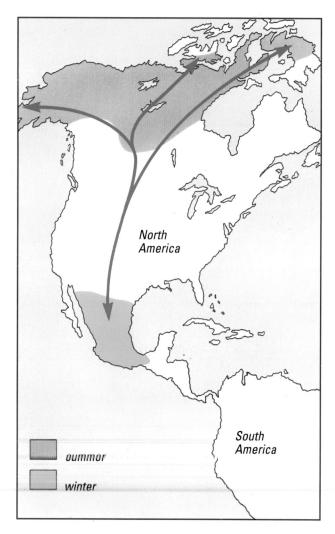

North America

South America

summer

winter

North American cranes are protected in their nesting areas and also where they spend the winter. But they need safe, undisturbed places during their long migration flights, too. The river beds where sandhill cranes have paused during thousands of years are being turned into farmland, and the cranes are finding it more and more difficult to feed and rest on their long journeys.

Sandhill cranes are among the most spectacular of migrating birds. Many thousands fly south each autumn from Alaska, northern Canada and the Great Lakes, to the southern USA. Their trumpeting calls can be heard well over a kilometre away, but sometimes flocks are so high that they can be heard but not seen from the ground.

White storks gather in great flocks at narrow sea crossings. They need to fly over warm land to glide on rising air currents and cannot fly far over water. Every autumn at places such as Gibraltar and the Bosphorus, all the storks from Europe gather to cross over to Africa.

OFF-COURSE RARITIES

With such speed and excitement in spring, some birds fly too far. They 'overshoot' instead of stopping at the right place. This sometimes means there are rare birds to see, such as hoopoes and bee-eaters, moving into northern France and southern England.

In autumn, things are more relaxed. Many birds stop to rest and feed up for days or even weeks, and there is less urgency about their journey. But there are also the young birds hatched that summer that face their first long-distance flights. They quite often get lost, drift off course in strong winds, or simply start out in the wrong direction.

REVERSE MIGRATION

This is one theory for rare birds such as Russian warblers turning up in strange places. They set off on the right 'line', but in the wrong direction, and reach western Europe instead of southeast Asia! These lost strays make autumn even better than the spring for seeing rare birds off course. But don't expect to find such rarities yourself. Most are a once-in-a-lifetime chance. If you do find one, it will be so much more exciting for being such a rare event.

Small warblers that are thousands of miles off course, such as this desert warbler, are fascinating rare birds - they really shouldn't be there at all!

Few rarities are so spectacular as the bee-eater. Common in southern Europe, it turns up in northern France and Britain only by accident, having flown too far north on its migration from Africa.

DIVING FOR A LIVING

masked booby

brown booby

common tern

scaup

guillemot

Many birds dive in water. Some, such as grebes and divers, swim along the surface and just 'disappear', sinking without a trace. Others, such as shags and coots, go under after taking a header, leaping forward and rolling under with a splash. There are some that dive in from a perch - kingfishers wait for a fish to show up, then dive headlong from an overhanging branch, or wire, or a jetty. Then there are those that dive from the air. Kingfishers do that, too. But the best examples are the terns, gannets and brown pelicans that fly over the water, looking down for fish, before plunging headlong with a loud splash.

All of them are after fish or other water creatures. A few species, such as gadwalls, don't dive but hang around diving coots and grebes and pick up scraps when they bring weed to the surface.

A trip to the sea is a good chance to watch some of these diving birds.

Not all kingfishers dive into water. African brown-hooded kingfishers dive from tree perches to catch insects.

European and American dippers are unusual songbirds that dive and even walk underwater. They don't have webbed feet and look nothing like ducks. Instead they are quite round and dumpy. But they live in fast streams and have big, strong feet that grip the bottom. They face into the current, leaning forward and slightly opening their wings so the force of the water pushes them down. They move about looking for caddis larvae and other water grubs.

common tern

brown pelican

guillemot

great northern diver

shearwater

cormorant

SPECIAL ADAPTATIONS

Some diving birds are specially fitted out for the job. Gannets dive in from 30 metres or more and hit the water with a terrific smack. It would hurt you or me! But they have cushions of air under the skin on the head and neck. The bones at the base of the bill are soft and spongy. The eyes are shielded by a tough membrane. Their nostrils close to keep the water out. And they have dense feathers all over their bodies. They are made for hitting water hard and not being knocked out.

UNDERWATER SWIMMERS

Many birds are designed to swim powerfully underwater. Webbed feet are frequent among the diving birds, but so are lobed toes. On the strong push backwards, the toes are spread apart to give the broadest possible webbing. On the forward stroke, the toes are closed and the webs fold up, to give the least resistance. Others swim with their wings instead of their feet. Guillemots can be watched under clear water from the top of their nesting cliffs. They swim with their wings, looking rather like seals with their big flippers.

Another seabird, the puffin, is better at 'flying' underwater. It chases fish by swimming with its wings. In the air, its wings are too small. It flies with a continuous, rapid whirr.

DIVING BIRDS

You can quickly build up an interesting project by timing the dives of the various ducks, grebes and coots at different ponds and lakes. When coots dive, they dive and come up in the same spot. Time their dives and try to get an idea of the water depth. Do they dive longer in deeper water? Do they bring food to the surface, or swallow it beneath the water? Grebes, goosanders and goldeneyes can move very long distances underwater and come up far from where you saw them first dive under - so watch carefully!

1 metre = 5 seconds

2 metres = 10 seconds

3 metres = 15 seconds

NIGHT BIRDS

Few of us go out in really black, deep night. Most of our nights are spoiled by street lights and the glow from distant towns. Therefore it is not easy to know what night is really like for a night bird far away from our homes. On the other hand, many night birds now have to put up with our lights, too.

NIGHTS AT SEA

Shearwaters and petrels are made for flight and swimming, and are so weak on land that in the light they are easy prey for big gulls. They come to their nesting burrows only at night - even a bright moon will put them off. In the pitch dark, they find their way by their sense of smell and by listening for the call of their mate on the nest. In very large colonies - often tens of thousands - it is amazing that any shearwater can recognize its mate's call in the noise.

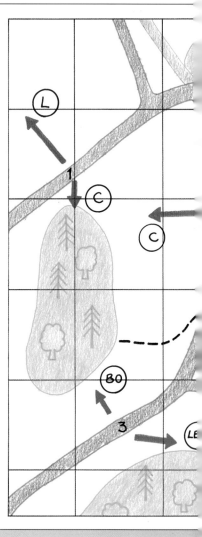

*BIRDS AT NIGHT
Oak Cottage Vale, Friday 12 June 1992, 9.30pm. There was a full moon, and no cloud. Light wind from east.*

1. At dusk, lapwings seen and heard in distance NW. Loud cuckoo in woods to S. Stayed 15 minutes.

2. Same cuckoo as at 1? calling continuously. Noisy call and flapping wings of disturbed pheasant N. Noisy mallards(?) flying over SE – probably flying to lake. Aircraft flew over. Stayed 20 minutes.

3. First barn owl of year called twice NW. Dad thinks he heard long-eared owl SE, only one call in distance. Stayed 15 minutes.

Home at 10.30pm.

If you know their songs and calls, you can survey birds at night. It's best to concentrate on a small area, well away from noisy traffic and buildings. Trace the main woods, roads and rivers of the area to be surveyed from a 1:25,000 map. You can then mark on what you hear at the places you stop at. Never go out alone at night.

Black skimmers feed by dragging the long tip of the lower half of their beak through water, ready to snap up fish. At night they make a trail through phosphorescent plankton which glow when disturbed. This attracts fish, so the skimmer turns around and goes back over its own track to catch them.

ACTIVITY AT NIGHT

LIGHT	TWILIGHT	DARK

Grasshopper warblers sing on moist, warm summer evenings

At dusk, the hobby catches moths; in the autumn, it will chase roosting swallows

Geese fly to roost, but may carry on feeding in moonlight

Woodlarks sing at dusk or later

Lapwings are still active into twilight, often calling at night

A barn owl will hunt early if it has a family to feed

Short-eared owls hunt in the evening after hen or marsh harriers have gone to roost

The nightjar comes out just after sunset, when moths are most active

Moorhens can be heard flying over at night, looking for new pools or ponds

The kestrel often hunts at dusk, the peak of vole activity

Cuckoos sing until dark in early summer

Tawny and long-eared owls wait for true darkness

The large-eyed stone-curlew begins to call at twilight, and flies to good feeding areas

Scops owls call from dusk, right through the night

The noisy oystercatcher's piping call can be heard beside northern coasts very late at night.

NIGHT-SIGHT

Can an owl see in the dark? Not really. It can see in dim light (but not very much better than we can), but its eyes are better at seeing detail in the dark than ours. Owls move around at night by knowing their home areas inside out, by using what they can make out with their eyes, and by using their sensitive ears which are specially made for pinpointing small sounds. Because owls' left and right ears are different sizes (and, often, one is higher than the other), they pick up sounds slightly differently, and so give a 3D effect to sound, comparable to what we see with our eyes. Some owls can even catch a mouse under a snowdrift, by hearing it squeak and diving at the sound.

Owls have neat fringes like fine hair along their feathers. This cuts down the noise their wings make and means they are silent in flight. They can hear their prey moving about, but the prey can't hear them coming.

BIRDS OF PREY

Often exciting and a treat to see, birds of prey are much misunderstood. Some are killers, at the top of the food chain - they are predators like lions and wolves, usually killing the weaker members of the species they prey on. But they rarely significantly reduce the numbers of their prey - it is usually the availability of prey that controls the predators. For example, if there are huge numbers of mice and voles, there will be more kestrels and owls to eat them. However, if the same kestrels and owls really reduced the numbers of prey, they themselves would starve. But they don't - over time, they reach a balance with their prey.

CARRION-EATERS
Many birds of prey, such as vultures and condors, eat carrion - animals that are already dead. They are scavengers, which may seem nasty, but they do a useful job by clearing away dead carcasses. Most carrion-eaters have long beaks and necks to probe among the carcasses. Even eagles eat a lot of carrion.

The sharp claws of a kestrel are perfect for catching voles and beetles. If necessary, the bill may be used to kill the captured prey.

THE BIRD-HUNTERS
Some falcons (such as the merlin and peregrine) and accipiters (such as the goshawk) are bird-hunters. They fly fast and look really exciting.

Goshawks live in the northern forests of North America, Europe and Asia. They ambush smaller birds, so they keep well out of sight. To see one you need to sit quietly by a forest clearing - and wait patiently! Small falcons (such as kestrels) are happy to eat small voles and beetles - and even buzzards sometimes eat worms, although they prefer rabbit.

American black vultures look for scraps or dead animals as they fly. If one spots food and descends, others follow it down. Soon large flocks gather as if from nowhere.

NIGHT HUNTERS

At night, another specialized bird of prey takes over - the owl. Many owls can survive only by knowing every last detail of their territories, and by having exclusive hunting rights there. If there are no other owls about, they can move around easily in the dark and find enough food. This is why owls spend so much of their time doing the rounds and 'singing' with their strange, hooting calls. They are telling other owls that 'this patch is occupied'.

HOW THEY HUNT

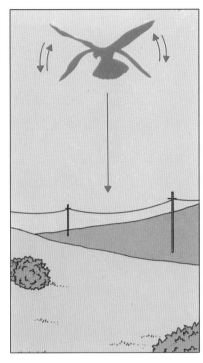

In the vast open wilderness where it hunts, the golden eagle has a good view but needs to dive fast to get close to its prey. It catches hares or grouse after a low, rapid chase close to the ground, or a steeper dive from high in the sky.

Watch a kestrel in its hover. Its body may move in the breeze, but its head keeps very still while it watches the ground below. If it spots something, it dives, perhaps pausing to check again half way down.

A pigeon might escape a peregrine in level flight, but the peregrine tries to soar up above its prey. Then it can drop in a lightning-fast dive and strike its prey with its feet. Few birds can escape it.

HUNTING GROUNDS

Because they prey on other birds and mammals, and need large and undisturbed hunting territories, the large eagles, hawks and falcons are always quite rare. There isn't enough food for them to be common. Therefore the commonest birds of prey are the ones which eat the more numerous rodents and insects.

POISON - A DEADLY BUSINESS

Crows and foxes, which are accused of killing gamebirds and chickens, are detested on many shooting estates and farms. Although the practice is illegal, poison is put out to kill them, in a dead rabbit or chicken 'bait'. Frequently, birds of prey, some of them endangered species, eat this poisoned bait, and are killed. Sometimes this killing is deliberate.

BIRDS OF THE OCEAN

The most remarkable thing about ocean birds is that they come back year after year to the same island or coastal cliff to nest. Imagine a tiny petrel - no bigger than a starling - flying low over the ocean waves for months on end. It may have travelled many thousands of kilometres. All it can see is the sky and a few metres of ocean around it. Yet each spring it not only finds the island where it nests, but even goes ashore at night and finds the very same burrow! Nobody can really explain how it is done.

STAYING ALOFT

Some ocean birds, incredibly, don't swim! Frigatebirds and sooty terns keep off the water, because their feathers would become waterlogged and they might sink. Instead, they fly thousands of kilometres across the oceans, soaring and gliding in the wind, never settling for an instant. They feed on fish at the water's surface, or even on flying fish, snatching them up in their bills.

You can see surprising numbers of birds from an ordinary ferry. Find a sheltered spot, where the deck doesn't vibrate too much. Keep scanning the sea with your binoculars. Don't look too far away from the ship - birds are mostly quite small! Sometimes a flock of gulls or terns will follow the ship.

SATELLITE TRACKING

Albatrosses have been caught and fitted with tiny transmitters and followed by satellite. They can travel 960 kilometres each day. They do it by gliding on the air currents that sweep upwards over big waves, and can only live in windy parts of the world. They are the ultimate ocean travellers.

GLIDING ON THE WIND

Wherever air rises, birds can stay airborne using very little energy. A wind off the sea rises above a cliff and gulls and fulmars can soar gracefully on the currents.

If a wind blows off the land, it falls over the cliff edge. However, the many swirling eddies create upcurrents which birds can still use to glide above the waves.

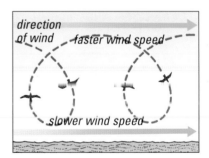

Simply by dragging across the waves, air is slowed down at the sea's surface. Shearwaters rise to the faster air above, to gain speed for their long glides downward.

Rows of whirring guillemots, screaming kittiwakes, wheeling gulls - busy cliffs, like this American Pacific coast one, have thriving birdlife like nowhere else.

Grey phalaropes are wading birds, but they often feed on the water rather than beside it. Instead of paddling in the shallows, they sit on the surface and pick up floating insects and tiny fish. They nest in the far north, mostly on the tundra where insects are abundant, but in winter they spend months out at sea. It seems a hard life for such delicate-looking birds.

LANDING TO NEST

Whatever the bird, it must come to land to nest. Most ocean birds choose rocky cliffs or islands, but some (such as tropical fairy terns and frigatebirds) nest in trees. Because their chicks take so long to grow, the big albatrosses may rear young only once every two years. Nearly all other birds nest every year. The small shearwaters and petrels also have enormously long breeding seasons, their eggs taking many weeks to hatch and their chicks just as long to develop. But many are very numerous, and so one compensation for their slow breeding is that there are many imma-ture birds not yet old enough to breed. If a disaster should strike a breeding colony, such as disease (or, nowadays, more likely an oil spill), there would still be some 'spare' birds out at sea to replace the losses.

tufted puffin

rhinoceros auklet

kittiwake

guillemot

pigeon guillemot

ancient murrelet

pelagic cormorant

Brandt's cormorant

western gull

black turnstone

black oystercatcher

BIRDS IN THE WOODS

In North America, red-headed woodpeckers store acorns and seeds under bark, to be eaten in times of shortage.

Not all birds live in trees, but those that do include some of the most common and familiar. It is worth investigating woods for rarer birds, too. What birds you see in woods depends on the kind of trees you get. Some birds can be found in almost any kind of trees, but others are much more likely to be in one or two sorts. To find your bird, learn its tree.

THE WONDERFUL OAK

The various oak trees of Europe and America have very many kinds of insects living on them. Beetles lay eggs under the bark, grubs tunnel in the wood, caterpillars eat the leaves, wasp larvae make galls. With so much to eat, many birds prefer oaks above all other trees. They are gnarled and rough, too, so they are great trees for places to nest. But specialists seek out other kinds. For example, beech trees produce masses of small nuts, called mast, in spiky pods. Chaffinches, hawfinches and great tits love them. Hawfinches go for hornbeam and cherries, too. Crossbills have beaks made for prising seeds out of cones, so they prefer spruce, pine and larch.

Woodland birds are specialized for life in a rich habitat. Getting at grubs in the wood, dealing with nuts and fruits and catching insects, all present new challenges for them.

Sapsuckers are American woodpeckers that bore holes in bark and eat the dripping sap, and also insects that are attracted to it.

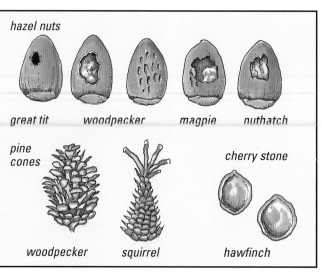

SIGNS OF FEEDING

It may be possible to detect the presence of birds even when they are nowhere to be seen. They leave behind signs which let us work out what they were eating. Split seeds, emptied nut cases, fallen pine cones, even holes probed into mud or chipped into fallen logs, all give us useful clues.

hazel nuts

great tit   woodpecker   magpie   nuthatch

pine cones

cherry stone

woodpecker   squirrel   hawfinch

In America and Europe, nuthatches leave several tell-tale signs. Nuts and berries wedged into crevices in tree bark, easier for pecking into, are typical nuthatch work.

66

America's flicker is a woodpecker, and, like the green woodpecker in Europe, it often eat ants.

The green woodpecker has a long tongue coiled around its skull. It can be pushed into ant hills to catch ants on its sticky, spiny tip.

The American brown creeper, very similar to European treecreepers, is difficult to spot on tree bark because of its streaked brown plumage.

To cover the biggest area of bark with the least effort, treecreepers start at the bottom of each tree and spiral upwards.

HABITAT VARIATION

It isn't just the food that affects the birds. Many nest in holes, so conifers in plantations are useless - they don't have holes! Pied flycatchers like open spaces beneath trees where they catch insects, so they go for woods where grazing animals keep down the brush underneath. Wood warblers nest in open spaces under tall dense trees, so they go for beeches with leaves so thick they cut out the light and nothing grows below them. Other birds like to live at the woodland edge, so you find more around ragged edges and beside clearings than you do in dense forest or along straight boundaries.

PATIENT TRACKING

Woodland birds are hard to see when trees are in leaf. You'll probably hear them first, then track them down. You see more at a pool where birds come to drink, so sit quietly and out of sight. In autumn, walk around until you find a mixed bird flock, then try to stick with it. Otherwise woods can seem empty.

THE DAWN CHORUS

Most brilliant singers are birds of the woods - the European nightingale, song thrush and blackcap are star performers; in North America, the hermit thrush and wood thrush take some beating. In spring and summer in the woods, go early, and go quietly, to hear the dawn chorus. All the forest birds sing loudly at daybreak, making a marvellous sound - you'll never forget it. Most birds will make themselves scarce when you arrive, but sit still and wait, and they will begin to move and sing again.

Later in the year you will hear the young birds calling to be fed. They scatter all through the trees, out of sight in the leaves. Some birds, such as pied flycatchers, just seem to disappear once their chicks have flown.

LAKES AND PONDS

All birds need water to drink, but some are specially suited to spend all their lives on or alongside water. Obvious ones are ducks and swans. Less well known are the grebes and divers and even some small birds such as kingfishers.

DUCKS

There are two main groups of freshwater ducks. The 'diving ducks' swim on the surface but dive under to feed. They eat underwater plants, water snails, shellfish or fish. In North America, common ones include redheads and ring-necked ducks; in Britain and Europe there are pochards and tufted ducks.

In winter, nearly all flocks of diving ducks will be mostly males, or mostly females. It is still not certain why they separate. In some ducks the males are bigger and stronger than the females, and migrate farther. This helps the species to survive better because they can spread out. It is not only ducks that do this. The scientific name of the chaffinch, *Fringilla coelebs*, means 'bachelor bird', and was used because males form separate flocks in winter.

Strange ducks often turn out to have escaped from zoos and wildlife parks, such as this brightly-coloured male mandarin.

WATERSIDE WATCH

Spring and autumn days beside a freshwater lake can be exciting. This is a good time to watch for migrants dropping in to feed for an hour or even a day or two - many of the rarest finds are shorebirds stopping beside reservoirs or along muddy edges of coastal pools.

Watching waterside birds needs care. If you go slowly and quietly to the water's edge, you are less likely to scare shy birds away.

Look in both directions as you approach, listening for bird calls, and try not to pop over banks or walls so that you are silhouetted against the sky. You may find wagtails, pipits and waders alongside the concrete slope of reservoirs.

The muddy shoreline may have teal, snipe and sandpipers on it. Quickly check the water, too: shy birds such as teal might fly off, while coots, grebes and cormorants will dive and swim away underwater.

teal

coots

great crested grebe

snipe

pied wagtail

common sandpiper

black-headed gulls

Over the water you will see many kinds of gulls, and maybe also terns. Black terns catch insects from the surface, while common terns plunge in for fish.

black terns

heron

edge warbler

kingfisher

In the reeds you might spot a kingfisher or a heron. Listen and watch for warblers in summer; in autumn, waterside reeds are used by swallows and wagtails for roosting - and huge flocks of starlings will dive into them to spend the night in safety.

reed warbler

SURFACE FEEDERS

The 'surface-feeding' ducks take floating plants and seeds from the surface of the water or mud, or just beneath it. They reach down by tilting over, or 'upending', or they filter food from the water with their special sieve-like bills. They include the mallard, gadwall and shoveler. Some of the surface feeders, such as the wigeon, are also 'grazers', eating grass on the shore.

With its broadly-lobed toes, the coot can walk on land, pecking at grass, swim on the surface, or dive underwater to get at nutritious water weeds.

GREBES AND COOTS

Grebes have such small legs so far back on their bodies that they are perfect swimmers but cannot walk. They don't have flattened bills like ducks, but dagger-like bills, more like herons. And their feet are not webbed, but have broad, flattened lobes along each toe. They eat fish, which they catch underwater. Coots, too, have lobed toes, and swim and dive, but they eat weed and come out to walk on dry land, to crop the grass. They are neither ducks nor grebes, but look a little like them. They are related to the rails, which creep about secretively in waterside vegetation and swamps.

WHERE THE RIVER MEETS THE SEA

A winding river with stands of reeds and willow thickets is a lovely place for a walk. Unfortunately, fewer rivers are now like this, as their banks have been cleared and beds straightened for better drainage. It makes them less varied and interesting for birds.

If you want to see lots of birds, go where two different habitats meet. At an estuary such as this North American one, you have the best of all worlds, land and sea, plus the shoreline itself.

ESTUARIES

It can be fascinating to walk down a river to its estuary, where it broadens out at the edge of the sea. There, the fresh, often muddy, water meets the salt sea, and twice-daily tides move salt water in and out along the river channel. It is a hard place to live, but many birds don't mind the changes.

Watch out for ducks. Some, such as mallards, live anywhere. Goosanders and mergansers nest by the river but fly out to sea. But scoters and eiders will be beyond the river mouth in the bay, and rarely come on to the fresh water.

Shorebirds increase as you approach the sea. The riverside is good for common sandpipers, as well as the occasional green sandpiper and greenshank. By the river mouth there will be more redshanks, oyster-catchers, dunlins and sanderlings.

American kestrel

osprey

boat-tailed grackles

American oystercatchers

bank swallows

eastern meadowlark

WHERE THE RIVER MEETS THE SEA

SALTMARSHES

Saltmarshes by river mouths are great places for birds. Gulls often nest in big colonies on the marsh. In wintertime, huge flocks of wildfowl - ducks and geese - and shorebirds feed in the muddy creeks and rest on the marsh at high tide.

ON THE SHORE

In summer look for common terns. They fish along some rivers, but mostly prefer the sea and nest along the shore. If you go near them while they are nesting, they will fly noisily around your head - so you can't miss them. But leave the area as quickly as you can. They are easily disturbed, and, while you keep them in the air, crows and gulls can snatch their eggs.

CHOOSE YOUR PATH

Use a good map if you walk along a river. It is easy to get cut off by a creek and have to walk a long way back to find a way around. Be especially careful near an estuary, and never go there without an adult. Tides race in very fast and can cut you off on mudbanks or strand you in the saltmarsh. If the tide is a big one, it can be deadly. Make sure you know the times of the tides, and don't go anywhere where you might have trouble getting back when the water rises.

HOLIDAY DIARY

If you go on a seaside holiday, you can keep a diary. Take colour photographs of the beach and the estuary and stick them in your book. Don't forget to include pictures of friends and family, too - you will enjoy looking at them in years to come.

As well as writing down all the birds you see, note which are on the river, which are on the sea, and which are in between. And as bird lists can be a bit dull on their own, don't be afraid to add to them. For example, if you had a fantastic view of a special bird at close range, in brilliant sunlight, say so. It will help bring back memories of your holiday and sightings when you read your diaries later.

Make a map of the estuary, showing the high-water and low-water levels, the area of sand, mud, shingle and marsh, and your regular walking routes. You can add even more detail, such as the direction of the sun and wind. Of course, don't forget to show where you see birds.

gulls and terns

goosander

common eiders

scaup

common scoters

song sparrow

sanderlings

willets

HIGH IN THE MOUNTAINS

Mountain birds are not easy to get to grips with but they are exciting. Treat them as a challenge, an ambition. Perhaps one day you will be on holiday in a mountain area and get a chance to see the variety of birds there for yourself.

UPLAND BIRDS

Actually there are more birds on 'uplands', the moors and hills below the stark mountain peaks. Moorland birds are still difficult to spot, because they live in low numbers on such vast areas of open space. They are hard to find and hard to get close to. You need to be at your best to stalk them, but some you will have to watch from a distance with a telescope.

BIG BIRDS OF PREY

Mountain birds include the spectacular golden eagle. It often circles the very highest peaks, going round in broad, slow arcs without beating its wings. Don't mistake buzzards for eagles. Buzzards are frequently lower down, and you can get much closer to them. You very rarely get close to an eagle.

BREEDING WADERS

Many birds which spend the winter on lowland fields or estuaries go to uplands to nest. In Britain, curlews and golden plovers nest on moorland slopes and in boggy valleys. Lapwings nest in the valley fields. In North America, the mountain plover is not a bird of mountain peaks, but nests on high, dry plains and plateaux and in semi-desert places.

Mountains are interesting places because you can study the changes in weather, vegetation and bird life as you climb from the bottom to the top. Going up is the same as going north, but the changes happen much more quickly. By the time you get to the top of some high, windswept, cold peaks, you feel as if you are in the Arctic! So do the birds.

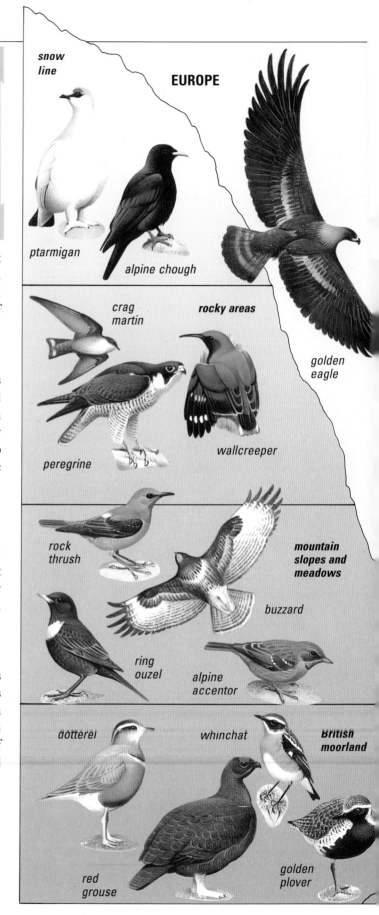

snow line

EUROPE

ptarmigan

alpine chough

crag martin

rocky areas

golden eagle

peregrine

wallcreeper

rock thrush

mountain slopes and meadows

buzzard

ring ouzel

alpine accentor

dotterel

whinchat

British moorland

red grouse

golden plover

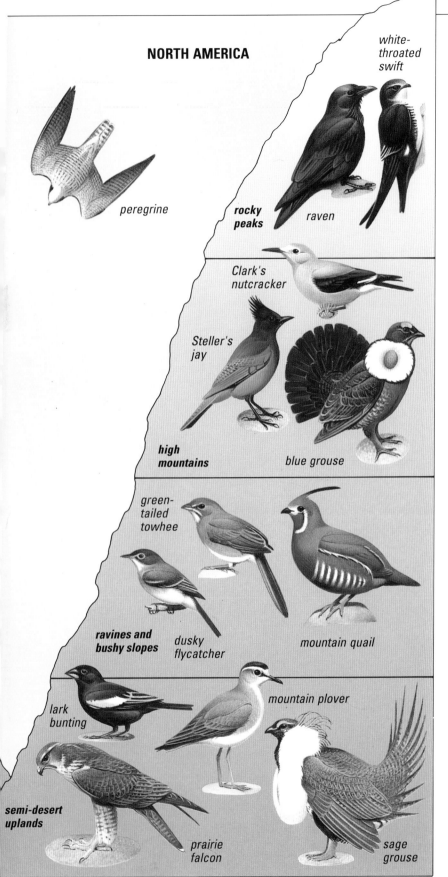

NORTH AMERICA

peregrine

white-throated swift

rocky peaks

raven

Clark's nutcracker

Steller's jay

high mountains

blue grouse

green-tailed towhee

ravines and bushy slopes

dusky flycatcher

mountain quail

lark bunting

mountain plover

semi-desert uplands

prairie falcon

sage grouse

SPECIAL GAMEBIRDS

Gamebirds live in all of the upland habitats. Red grouse are birds of high British heather moors, while willow grouse are Arctic birds in Northern Scandinavia and North America. The ptarmigan lives on the highest peaks and Arctic tundra, whereas mountain quails live on high bushy slopes in the North American Rockies. Sage grouse prefer sagebrush in the foothills, while prairie chickens are rare and declining in the remnants of tall-grass prairies.

MOUNTAIN FIELDCRAFT

It is vital to be safe and comfortable on a hike or climb in mountains and hills. All walkers should always tell people where they are going and when they will be back. Check the weather forecasts, and never set off if bad weather is predicted. Wear the proper clothes and take extra layers with you. Take plenty of food and drink, maps and a compass. And be careful! Mountains and moors can be dangerous places.

ALWAYS VIGILANT
Be on the lookout for birds as soon as you get to the mountains. A few birds are relatively tame, and can even be found around car parks. Flocks of alpine choughs are regular visitors to European ski stations.

SOLID FOOTHOLDS
Never go close to the edges of cliffs or scree slopes, which could give way beneath you - there will be plenty of safe paths and viewpoints on your route. Even grassy slopes can be very slippery, so don't be tempted to creep down them.

ADVANCING YOUR HOBBY

The best and most expert birdwatchers live their whole lives aware of birds. They watch them from the house, from the car, from trains, from the office. Birds are everywhere, so there is no chance to stop! You, too, can become a top birder, or even an expert ornithologist - a scientist who really studies birds - but it takes time to get the knowledge and experience. For example, ringing, or banding, birds by catching them and attaching tiny, numbered rings on their legs is a job for a highly-trained specialist. You need a licence to do it.

GETTING INTO BIRD STUDIES

With birds in the garden or park, or around the local lake, there is plenty of subject matter. All you need is to set yourself some targets. You can do several projects at once, as part of your normal birdwatching. The basis is keeping good notes, which you can analyze later. Start by concentrating on one area with good birds - maybe a reservoir or a wood. Keep notes of what you see, when, and how many.

A MARK OF DISTINCTION

Bewick's swans in England have been studied by making detailed drawings of their face patterns. Every one is recognizable. Maybe you can recognize some birds by their own individual marks?

Most local societies carry out work to protect and develop habitats for birds and other wildlife. For example, cutting scrub or clearing rubbish from ponds is valuable work.

Cleaning oiled seabirds is not a job for the amateur or beginner. If you find an oiled bird, it is essential to seek expert advice if you wish to help it.

BIRDSONG STUDIES

A diary of birdsong could be your project. You can relate it to the weather. Do birds sing earlier in the mornings in spring or in autumn? Do more sing at dusk in the summer? There is a lot to be discovered.

If you observe birds singing and displaying, you can make maps of breeding birds holding territories. These are the basis of census work - maps showing symbols for each species, whether they were males singing, or fighting, or displaying to females, or females taking food to young. Major conservation organizations use such censuses to plan their efforts to protect wildlife throughout the world.

MIGRATION WATCH

Woods and waterside places are great for seeing migrants arrive in spring. It is easy to record the first you see of every summer visitor, each year. It is harder to keep good records of the last you see! Keep a chart of migrant arrival and departure dates. Look at your local bird club reports, and see how your dates compare with others. Send your notes in to the local recorder so they can be added to the report.

These are some ideas, but your local situation will help suggest some lines of study that are worth following, too. Whatever you do, have fun!

On many nature reserves, bird boxes are put up to attract birds to nest there. Occasionally, the boxes are checked by wardens to see if they are being used, and to record the breeding numbers for a census. Perhaps you can help - but *never* look in bird boxes unless supervised by an expert.

SOME PROJECT IDEAS

Check out nest sites of house martins. Which direction do they face? Are there more on white-painted house eaves than on any other colour? But do you think that is just because there is more white paint on houses? Do they like new houses or old ones?

Watch big gulls. You can see when they start to moult and when they finish many weeks later. Keep a chart of their moult timing. You will find that old birds moult at different times from young ones.

In autumn, birds eat berries. Find out what types of berries are around. See which birds eat them, and which are left until later. What happens in winter if it snows?

Making maps of birds' territories is a good project. It is easiest to do this with birds which sing or display distinctively, or have eyecatching colours, such as this female stonechat on a prominent perch.

INDEX